France / NAPoleon

1395

950

D0554826

950

NAPOLEON'S ENEMIES

1 Prime & Load

NAPOLEON'S ENEMIES

Edited by RICHARD WARNER

With a foreword by David Chandler

2 Handle Cartridge   3 Prime

Osprey Publishing, London

Published in 1977 by
Osprey Publishing Ltd.
12–14 Long Acre, London WC2E 9LP
Member company of the George Philip Group

ISBN 0 85045 172 8

Filmset by BAS Printers Limited, Wallop, Hampshire
and printed by Ebenezer Baylis and Son, Ltd.,
The Trinity Press, Worcester, and London

4 Load

Acknowledgement

Much factual information, some half-tones, and many colour plates have been taken from books in the Men-at-Arms series, describing the armies which fought against Napoleon. I am very grateful to the authors and artists concerned for the material provided.

I should like to thank Freda Marsh for making order out of chaos without a sigh.

R.W.

For Philip Warner

6 Draw Ramrod

Contents

6 Ram down Cartridge

Illustrations

Foreword
by David Chandler

'Between old monarchies and a young republic the spirit of hostility must always exist,' remarked Napoleon Bonaparte at the time of the Peace of Amiens in 1802. 'In the present state of affairs every peace treaty means no more than a brief armistice; and I believe that my destiny will be to fight almost continuously.' The First Consul's forecast was to prove all too correct. Ten years of continuous warfare had already stretched France's resources since the fateful day of 20 April 1792, when the idealistic Girondin government had declared war on 'the King of Hungary and Bohemia' (the secondary titles of the Austrian Emperor) in a fit of patriotic revolutionary fervour, thus inaugurating the long French Revolutionary and Napoleonic Wars. But the long campaigns against the First and Second Coalitions were to prove only the introduction. The fourteen month breathing spell represented by the duration of the Peace of Amiens did indeed prove no more than a 'brief armistice', serving to usher in a further eleven years of mounting conflicts, involving a succession of four more hostile coalitions, before Napoleon was induced to abdicate for the first time at Fontainebleau; and even then there would remain the dramatic events of the Hundred Days (which called into being the Seventh Coalition) before an exhausted Europe could settle down at long last to a period of peace and reconstruction.

The true cost of this period of devastating wars will never be known. In terms of casualties, it has been estimated that France and her more or less willing confederates lost all of 1,750,000 killed and wounded between March 1804 and June 1815. If the unknown losses of France's opponents and of the preceding Revolutionary Wars are also taken into account, a

total in the region of five million casualties might not be excessive.

Historians have spent much effort apportioning the responsibility for these appalling circumstances, and those who have tried to show that the major blame should be placed at Napoleon's door have proved as unconvincing as those who have sought to demonstrate that France and its dynamic ruler were the hapless victims of an international conspiracy. In sober fact, the period was distinctly war-prone from its outset, and there is every likelihood that Europe would have been torn by major conflicts whether or not Napoleon Bonaparte had appeared on the scene. For the Revolution had set France apart from the rest of Europe while the future Emperor was still an unknown lieutenant of artillery. The social and economic upheavals that followed the act of political defiance in 1789 implied the end of the *Ancien Régime* – not only in France but throughout the Continent. The old monarchies were bound to resist to the uttermost the concepts of Rousseau and Diderot, for the vaunted slogan of *Liberté, Egalité et Fraternité* threatened a total upheaval of European society and the destruction of most vested interests. They also signalled the liberation of a great burst of nationalistic energy and proselytising zeal amongst the French people – and this phenomenon was bound to lead to expansionist wars whether or not Napoleon had emerged to lead the nation.

It mattered little that the form of French government swung all the way from an extremist regicide republic to a continental empire, for the implicit menace was much the same. The crowned heads of Europe – Austrian Habsburgs, Spanish and Neapolitan Bourbons, Russian Romanovs and British

Hanoverians – could no more trust the 'Corsican adventurer' who was prepared to have the noble Duc d'Enghien kidnapped from neutral territory and shot with his back to a wall at the Chateau de Vincennes in March 1804, than they could respect the memory of his revolutionary predecessors who had dragged Louis XVI and his queen beneath the blade of the guillotine in 1793. They might be temporarily lured into 'compacts with the devil' for reasons of military necessity, dynastic interest or personal fascination – but no such agreements held a stamp of true permanence for Napoleon was an outsider and indeed an outlaw, or such was the view of most of the old-established régimes of Europe. The British government, for example, never acknowledged his assumed imperial rank, but referred to him as 'General Bonaparte' in all official pronouncements and documents until after his death. And it is also significant that Napoleon found no acceptance from *les grandes dames* of European monarchy. The implacable hostility of the Dowager-Empress of Russia, the Empress Ludovica of Austria and Queen Louise of Prussia was a factor not to be ignored, for their influence over their sons or husbands was immense.

Of course to a large extent Napoleon played into the hands of his reactionary opponents. He did not play the diplomatic game with the utmost tact, that elusive 'golden quality' of statesmanship. There was little time for compromise in his Corsican nature, despite the cunning and opportunism he displayed on certain occasions. All too often the treaties and pacifications he initiated were little more than dictated peaces. The self-confident and arrogant tone of French negotiators and the pronouncements of their master inevitably gave much offence and exacerbated international relations. His terms for amiable relations were always high in terms of extracted concessions, men to swell the ranks of the Empire's armies and money to pay for their food and munitions. Thus no ex-enemy could be converted into a convinced confederate, and even his genuine allies were often reduced to the status of resentful satellites and exploited vassals.

This notwithstanding, it is improbable that the latent power of the new France and the genius that came to the head of its government and armies at the turn of the century would have been baulked and ultimately defeated by the European monarchies had not the Great Britain of George III taken the lead of the opposition. Time and again the continental armies would be crushingly defeated by French arms in successive wars and campaigns, but their eclipse in each case proved transitory. That this was the case was largely due to the steady hostility evinced by successive British ministries from 1793, the security provided by the Royal Navy and the Channel – obstacles that Napoleon was never able to tame – and the considerable national wealth that Britain was prepared to distribute in the form of subsidies to her continental allies in return for their adherence to fresh coalitions designed to challenge and thwart French purposes. From 1793 to 1806 the prime mover behind British policy was William Pitt the Younger, whether in office as prime minister or working behind the scenes. He was the architect of the Second and Third Coalitions – and it was the collapse of the latter after the battle of Austerlitz that reputedly hastened his own death the following spring. Nevertheless his successors took over Pitt's policies and general approach to the European scene, and his influence may be said to have continued to inspire British and continental hostility to Napoleon for years after his disappearance from the scene.

The earlier coalitions were very ramshackle affairs, undermined by selfish national interests and inconsistent war aims. The First Coalition (1792–7) – which Britain joined rather than inspired – was bedevilled by Austrian and Prussian friction over Poland, and lacked co-ordination. 'Their aims being as diverse as their methods were disputed,' wrote Professor J. Holland-Rose, 'the term, "First Coalition" applied to this league is almost a misnomer.' It began to fall apart in early 1795, and Tuscany, Prussia and Sardinia made separate peaces with France over the next 18 months, and it finally collapsed when Austria signed the Peace of Campo Formio in October 1797. The Second Coalition lasted from 1798 until the Peace of Amiens, involving Britain, Austria, Russia, Naples and Turkey, and again lack of proper co-ordination led to military failure and diplomatic humiliation. The Third (April to December 1805) was very short-lived. The fact that the Austrians and Russians did not fully realise that their two countries were employing different calendars – a factor of great significance during the Ulm and Austerlitz campaigns, particularly at the start – gives some measure of the general inefficiency of these compacts. The Fourth Coalition, formed by

Britain, Prussia and Russia from July 1806, crashed in ruins after Jena-Auerstadt in the face of Napoleonic *blitzkrieg*, but the ghost lingered on until the Tilsit agreements of July 1807, which again left Britain isolated. The so-called Fifth Coalition (April to October 1809) brought Britain and Austria into brief alliance – until the defeat of Wagram led to Austria's Treaty of Vienna with France.

Only with the Sixth Coalition, which first came into existence in July 1812 and survived intact until Napoleon's first abdication on 16 April, 1814, did a truly effective alliance emerge. Great Britain, Russia, Spain and Portugal were the original participants, but they were ultimately joined by Prussia and Austria by mid-1813, and by other German states as the bounds of the Napoleonic Empire recoiled towards the Rhine. Single-mindedness and a common purpose were written into such agreements as the Treaty of Chaumont (9 March 1814) by which all the signatories solemnly undertook to commit all their national resources to the war, to enter into no separate treaties or negotiations with Napoleon, and to form a post-war Congress which would tackle the problems of Europe. If necessary, these obligations were to last for a full 20 years.

The Congress of Vienna was, of course, in somewhat acrimonious session considering the re-organisation of post-war Europe when the news of Napoleon's return from Elba exploded like a bomb-shell. On 25 March 1815 all the signatories of the former Sixth Coalition reaffirmed the terms of Chaumont, outlawed Napoleon, and joined together in the Seventh Coalition, dedicated to pursuing all-out war against Napoleon until his final eclipse was assured. This came on 18 June long before the full weight of the Austrian and Russian military power could be brought to bear, but in the event the Anglo-Dutch and Prussian armies of Wellington and Blücher proved equal to the challenge, and Napoleon's last desperate gamble collapsed in resounding failure. Thus in the end the European powers learnt how to co-operate effectively against a common foe, but as we have indicated the necessary lessons were only slowly assimilated over two decades of failure and humiliation. Only Great Britain can be said to have shown true singleness of purpose from 1803 onwards, and but for her determination to bring Napoleon down, and her willingness to back her diplomatic undertakings with large sums of money, it

seems unlikely that an effective and properly cohesive alliance would ever have emerged.

Of course, diplomatic considerations alone would never have defeated Napoleon unless there had been proper military backing to provide the teeth. The successive failure of five coalitions was as closely linked to the inadequacies of the forces the participants were compelled to deploy in the field as it was to their common rivalries and selfish national interests. This book pays attention to the armies that emerged from the hard school of experience. Apart from the British Army, which developed along its own lines, the major continental forces chose to remodel themselves along adaptations of Napoleon's *Grande Armée*, adopting the army corps system and other salient features to good effect. The Archduke Charles of Austria, Scharnhorst in Prussia and Barclay de Tolly in Russia proved capable of borrowing the best French organisational and tactical concepts, and applying them to their own reformed armies. The processes of modernisation were often painful and were opposed by strong local vested interests, but the lessons of Austerlitz, Jena and Friedland could not be ignored, and within a decade Austria, Prussia and Russia had abandoned most of the facets of 18th century warfare and brought their armies up to date. In many ways the British army did not share in these developments. The humiliations suffered during the American War of Independence had already led to some long overdue reforms: Sir David Dundas overhauled and standardised the system of line infantry tactics, Sir John Moore reintroduced light infantry and his influence began to improve officer-man relationships within the regiments, and the Duke of York proved an administrator of considerable skill. But, as this book brings out, the real strength of the British army lay in its individual regiments, and these proved more than a match for the conscripts of the French army in many a Peninsular engagement. The British army receives pride of place in the pages that follow, and that is right; but it is also correct that space is found for the consideration of certain aspects of the armies of our continental allies which rose like the phoenix from the ashes of military defeat and demonstrated the possibilities of international co-operation. Not even the genius of Napoleon could ultimately withstand the combined pressure of his united adversaries.

I
TACTICS OF WAR

Historical background

In the early eighteenth century, wars had generally been fought for limited objectives, and wars of position were more common than wars of movement. A complete defeat of the enemy was believed to be beyond the means of any state; the method was a war of attrition, and the aim the seizure of fortresses and key points to put one side or other in a stronger position to bargain at the peace conference.

The tactics of the day were dominated by the use of the smooth-bore musket, and the pike or bayonet; the musket, in spite of its short range, inaccuracy and slowness of fire, could be decisive if fired in concentration and in volley. The normal order of battle for musketeers was in line three or four ranks deep, and the deployment and movement involved had to be learned on the parade-ground by professional troops who devoted their lives to the service. Such professional soldiers were valuable and were not to be squandered, and Austrian generals in particular became a byword for prudence, believing that it was better to preserve their own troops than to destroy those of the enemy. The great Field-Marshal Daun was the protagonist of the creed that the defence was stronger then the offence; nor, even when pitted against a general of Frederick the Great's calibre, was he necessarily proved wrong. For he defeated Frederick on successive occasions, using the stonewall tactics of the period.

The French Army had declined since its golden age under Louis XIV, and it was left to Frederick the Great to change military thinking from the middle of the century onwards. For Frederick believed only in the attack, whatever the odds, and his audacity, coupled with mobility of movement, won him battle after battle. Yet in many respects even Frederick was

of the old school. He maintained the efficiency of his officer corps by personal example, by rigorous energy, and by meticulous inquiry, but even he took his officers from the nobility and not from the bourgeoisie: only rarely did he commission soldiers from the ranks. Close-order drill remained the safeguard of battle efficiency and, although he was not, on occasions, averse to eating bare the countryside of an enemy, he relied for supplies on an elaborate system of fortresses, state magazines, depots, and supply convoys, and was unwilling to venture his armies more than four days' march from a supply base or over twenty miles from a navigable river. His troops, like those of his enemies, remained long-service professional soldiers, although they were sometimes reinforced by mercenaries, by the enforced conscription of prisoners, and by national levies. It was Frederick's tactics and methods that were original, not his philosophy. And the Austrians learned much from him which they turned to good advantage during the Seven Years War.

From 1792 onwards the whole concept of warfare was radically changed by the French revolutionaries, for it was waged more ruthlessly and more efficiently as a conflict of ideologies.

The French royalist artillery and engineer corps had remained in being, together with most of its officer corps. The main body of the old infantry and cavalry had largely disappeared, however, and the new armies were formed by the *levée en masse*, a compulsory conscription of the nation's youth. Since there was no time to train the new recruits in the old methods of deployment into line of battle, the revolutionaries devised their own tactic of a column advance, with fixed bayonets, to overwhelm an enemy line. A single battalion had a frontage of forty

This general's rank is shown by the even spacing of the loops (false buttonholes) on the lapels, cuffs, and the tails of his coatee. On active service his cocked hat would be worn fore and aft. (Roffe/Osprey)

brought heavy losses to the French, but as men were plentiful and lives were cheap, this was considered of little account. Fear of the guillotine, the penalty for failure by officers, ensured that commanders were energetic; the reward of promotion was all the more immediate because of the high number of casualties.

One might imagine that the French tactics would spell disaster: the Austrian, Prussian, and Russian veterans found that this was not so, being rapidly swept away by the conscript columns of France. Why were the French so effective? The closed ranks made control easier; no man could falter or run away once in formation. The column's advance was covered by artillery at the flank and skirmishers in front, who tried to break the enemy line of fire before the arrival of the main body. The effect on enemy morale of the steady advance of massed columns accompanied by artillery fire and the constant nagging of the skirmishers before the battle was properly joined also helped the French, convinced as they were of their invincibility. Finally, idealism, a poor factor on its own, but a powerful one when combined with confidence and strength, could give the re-volutionaries the edge when resisted: Napoleon was quick to recognize and use this quality, unaffected as he was by it himself.

Alone of Bonaparte's opponents, Britain resisted the change to column attack which had brought France such great success, having the steadiness and temperament to sustain the bludgeon attacks.

The French army at this time was superior to its enemies in organization, armament, and offensive spirit. Promotion depended on merit not birth. Morale, after the suppression of the extremist revolutionaries, was excellent, and Napoleon was little plagued by desertion – the curse of his enemies' long-service armies.

Napoleon himself was enormously popular with his troops. Still there was much of the charlatan about him. With his remark, 'What do the lives of half a million men matter to a man like me?' he certainly was not averse to the shedding of blood. Yet he lost more men in his rapid marches than he did in battle. For he was the strategist *par excellence*; the unfortunate Mack had been forced to surrender at Ulm in 1805 because no Austrian could conceive it possible that the Grande Armée could march from Boulogne to the Danube, a distance of nearly 700 miles, in under eight weeks.

men and a depth of twenty-four ranks; more battalions could give greater frontage and depth. When ordered to attack, the battalion marched to the beat of the drum in serried ranks, rather like a phalanx or square, direct on to the enemy. There was no question of any use of musketry since the assault formation did not allow it; the men of the first two ranks might fire a round on closing with the enemy, but this was done on the move, and the rapid march-step allowed no time to reload. Such attacks, in reality nothing more than marching right over the enemy,

Since the French revolutionaries could not afford to provide magazines and baggage-trains for their troops, the armies were ordered to live off the land; to do this they had to keep moving, preferably in the direction of the enemy. Napoleon continued the system, applying it, if anything, more ruthlessly. In the early years it enhanced his mobility; in Russia it destroyed his army. Bonaparte in his prime had no peer as a soldier, but his failure to delegate responsibility led to lack of initiative in his subordinates. Trusting overmuch to his star, he eventually became careless in reckoning the strength of his opposition. Much of his success was due to the boldness of his plans and the simplicity and speed with which he executed them. He relied heavily on the excellent marching powers of his troops, and the advantage of surprise that this provided. As a tactician, on the other hand, his only great contribution was in his skilful use of artillery – the arm in which he had started his career. He remained faithful

A staff officer busy with plans. His branch of the service is shown by the silver facings on his uniform. (Roffe/Osprey)

to the method of attacking in column which had brought so much early success, even though his marshals had been defeated using the tactic in the Peninsula. At Waterloo he was finally defeated, still trusting in the column method, which had been bequeathed to him by Carnot.

The Infantry

When Wellington took the field in the Peninsula in 1808, Britain lagged behind France in the higher organization of her armies, divisions had yet to be formed, and Wellington dealt direct with individual brigade commanders. In June 1809, however, he adopted the divisional organization originated by the French, in which a number of brigades were grouped together under a single commander. Initially he formed four divisions, but by 1812 the number had risen to eight British and one Portuguese; he numbered his British divisions consecutively from one to seven; the eighth, the most famous, was known simply as the Light Division. Each was commanded by a lieutenant-general and usually comprised three brigades, two of which were British, each under a major-general, and one foreign, often under a British brigadier-general – a rank otherwise seldom encountered in the Peninsular Army.

There were some exceptions. All three brigades of the 2nd Division were British, but since it normally operated with General Hamilton's Portuguese Division, both under the command of Wellington's most trusted subordinate, General 'Daddy' Hill, the two together virtually amounted to the equivalent of a small Anglo-Portuguese army corps. In the 1st Division the foreign brigade was from the King's German Legion, recruited by George III from the remnants of his Hanoverian Army; in the remainder (except for the Light Division which had a peculiar organization of its own) it came from the Portuguese Army which had been reorganized under the command of Marshal Beresford and stiffened by British officers who had transferred to the Portuguese service.

The composition of the Light Division derived from an essential feature of Wellington's tactics. He had served under the Duke of York in Flanders where he had noted how the French light troops, their *Tirailleurs* and *Voltigeurs*, could harass and weaken a battle line, so that when the heavy French columns attacked it they often broke through. He resolved to counter this gambit by deploying forward of his positions such a mass of his own light troops that the *Tirailleurs* and *Voltigeurs* would be held well short of his main position. As a first step towards achieving this aim, he constituted the Light Division with the function of screening the army both at rest and on the move. It consisted of only two small brigades each containing a *Caçadore* battalion (Portuguese Light Infantry), four companies of riflemen from the 95th (later increased when the 2nd and 3rd battalions of that regiment joined his army), and a British light infantry battalion (the role in which the 43rd and 52nd won immortal fame).

The 7th Division also was rather unusual; perhaps at first Wellington toyed with the idea of producing another light infantry division. It had two light infantry brigades, one containing two light battalions of the King's German Legion and nine rifle companies of the Brunswick-Oels Jägers, and the other two newly-trained British light infantry battalions, the 51st and the 68th, and a battalion originally recruited from French *emigrés* and deserters, the Chasseurs Britanniques, a regiment famous for the speed with which its men deserted. In addition there was the normal Portuguese brigade. This division, perhaps owing to its diversity of races, never won much renown; the malicious affected to disbelieve in its very existence, and in 1813 it reverted to a more normal organization, the light infantry battalions from the King's German Legion being transferred to the 1st Division.

In the British brigades there were generally three line battalions. Occasionally a fourth might be added, and in Guards Brigades, since a battalion of Foot Guards invariably outnumbered by a considerable margin those of the line, there were only two. On average a brigade numbered about 2,000 men, but sickness and casualties, or the arrival of a strong battalion, could cause wide fluctuations. The Portuguese brigades followed the Continental model and embodied a *Caçadore* battalion and two line regiments each of two battalions; these had seven companies and an authorized strength of 750, but rarely put more than 500 in the field. Even so, Portuguese brigades on average numbered 2,500 and were almost always larger than the British.

The organization of the British battalions remained remarkably constant throughout the war. Each was commanded by a lieutenant-colonel and consisted of a grenadier company, a light company, and eight line companies, all commanded by captains. The colonel had two majors serving under him, nominally to command the two wings into which the battalion was customarily split. Their main function, however, was to deputize for him when he was away and to take charge of any large detachments the battalion might be called upon to make. Within the battalion their duties tended to depend on the particular whims or eccentricities of their commanders.

Wellington had with him two senior generals whom he could send off at a moment's notice to take over an independent command or disentangle some unfortunate situation; it gave him a flexibility that allowed him to dispense with the system of Army Corps originated by the French.

On the civil side there was an important department, the Commissariat, under a Commissary-General with assistants serving with every division and brigade. These were responsible for the provision of rations and the procurement of all local produce. In the nature of things a thin or ill-provided commissary officer was rarely seen, and they were apt to receive more kicks than credit.

Working direct to Army Headquarters were the divisions; there was only an intermediate headquarters when two or more were grouped together for an independent task. Here staffs were kept to the minimum. Leith Hay (later to become lieutenant-colonel and author of *A Narrative of the Peninsular War*), an ADC with the 5th Division, records that at the Battle of Salamanca the divisional staff consisted of Colonel Berkeley, probably Assistant-Quarter-Master-General, and Major Gomm, probably Deputy-Assistant-Adjutant-General, and four ADCs, possibly one per brigade and one to look after the domestic arrangements of the headquarters. The high-sounding titles for staff officers have been retained to the present day, generally abbreviated to the initials, thereby ensuring that the army staff should be confusing to the other services and incomprehensible to other nations.

At the level of the infantry brigade, there was a single staff officer, the major of brigade; he was a captain or sometimes an able young subaltern drawn from one of its regiments. During the later stages of the war, when regimental officers had recognized the wisdom of wearing the same type of headdress as their

men, staff officers could be distinguished by their courageous refusal to abandon the traditional cocked hat.

In the companies, the captains had under them two junior officers, in theory a lieutenant and an ensign, but there was no set ratio of one rank to the other. A full-strength battalion, therefore, would be commanded by a lieutenant-colonel with under him two majors, ten captains, twenty lieutenants or ensigns, the adjutant, (generally a lieutenant), and the quartermaster; an assistant surgeon was normally attached. Sir David Dundas shows the strength of a company as being three officers, two sergeants, three corporals, one drummer, and thirty privates. This must have been at the peacetime establishment of one platoon. At war establishment, another platoon was added without any increase in the number of officers. When going to the Peninsula, companies might number nearly 100, including a pay sergeant, perhaps four other sergeants, and six corporals. The 52nd went to the Peninsula with fifty-four sergeants and about 850 rank and file. But sickness and other casualties soon took their toll, and when in 1810 the 2nd battalion of the 52nd disbanded, its total strength was twenty sergeants, twelve buglers, and 572 rank and file, of whom ten sergeants, five buglers, and eighty-five rank and file were unfit for duty.

A battalion with 700 men present in the field was looked on as strong; many fell well below this figure; and some had little more than 500. In a battalion of 700 men, deducting the musicians, the adjutant's batman, the clerks, the storemen, and others of that ilk likely to find their way into headquarters – say forty men – there would be 660 men serving with the companies; allowing again for the various duties that inexorably sap the strength of a regiment such as baggage-guards, storemen, men just gone sick, absentees, and so on, the company could probably put not much more than fifty-five men into the line. Captain Sherer (later Major M. Sherer, author of *Recollections of the Peninsula*) remarked that at the Battle of Vitoria he had eleven casualties out of a company of thirty-eight and does not comment that at this time his company strength was abnormally low. The company for administrative purposes was divided into two platoons, but organizations were far from standardized, and commanding officers were often men of character who liked to run their battalions after their own fashion and did not welcome interference from the nincompoops of the staff. The private soldier in the ranks carried sixty rounds of ball ammunition, a knapsack, a haversack, rolled blanket or greatcoat, a full waterbottle, and probably some other articles he had managed to acquire; his load might amount to nearly sixty pounds. At first the heavy camp-kettles for cooking were carried on a company mule, but when, in 1812, Wellington managed to issue tents to his men at a scale of three twelve-men bell-tents per company, the

This infantry officer in a Line Regiment is wearing his cold weather uniform. His stovepipe shako is protected by an oilskin cover, of which the flap shows. The waist sash shows he is an officer. (Roffe/Osprey)

This field officer of the 7th Foot (Royal Fusiliers) wears two epaulettes. He has the blue facings – which distinguished all 'royal' regiments – and a fur cap. The fusiliers had originally been formed for the purpose of escorting the artillery and were then armed with the flintlock fusil. (Roffe/Osprey)

tents were carried on the mule and a lighter type of camp-kettle was carried in turn by the men of the company.

The 'Brown Bess'

Officers were armed with the sword, and sergeants with halberds or short pikes, called spontoons, rather to assist them in dressing the ranks than as weapons of offence. Most of the soldiers were armed with the musket, affectionately known as Brown Bess, that the Duke of Marlborough, when Master-General of the Ordnance, was said to have introduced. Its barrel was

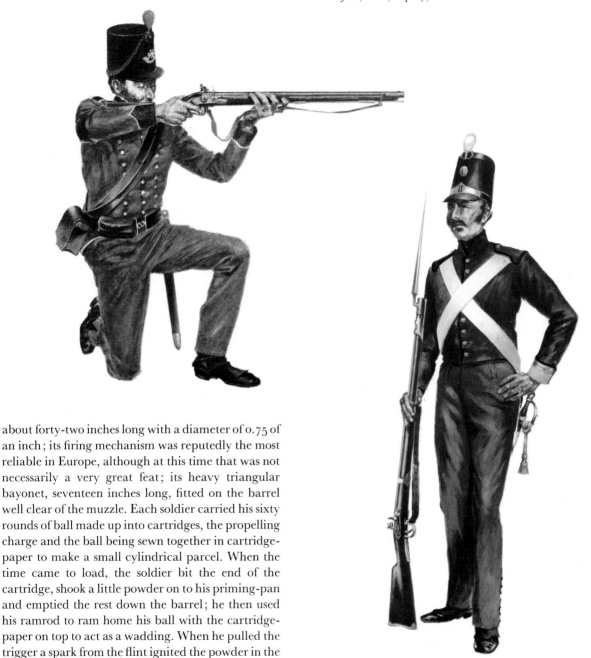

This rifleman of the 95th Foot (The Rifle Brigade) wears the dark green uniform of the huntsman. Note his black collar, cuffs, and shoulder straps, outlined in white braid. He is aiming the Baker Rifle. (Roffe/Osprey)

about forty-two inches long with a diameter of 0.75 of an inch; its firing mechanism was reputedly the most reliable in Europe, although at this time that was not necessarily a very great feat; its heavy triangular bayonet, seventeen inches long, fitted on the barrel well clear of the muzzle. Each soldier carried his sixty rounds of ball made up into cartridges, the propelling charge and the ball being sewn together in cartridge-paper to make a small cylindrical parcel. When the time came to load, the soldier bit the end of the cartridge, shook a little powder on to his priming-pan and emptied the rest down the barrel; he then used his ramrod to ram home his ball with the cartridge-paper on top to act as a wadding. When he pulled the trigger a spark from the flint ignited the powder in the pan which in turn caused the powder in the barrel to explode; the proportion of misfires, however, could be as high as one in six and, if the powder became damp, the musket would not fire at all.

This corporal in the Portuguese infantry is wearing the normal blue coatee of the Portuguese army although this was probably manufactured in England. His rank is shown by the double gold stripe round the cuff. (Roffe/Osprey)

The ball was not always a very close fit in the barrel, and the gases from the exploding charge might escape around it making it spin and swerve wildly in flight. Brown Bess had a certain feminine capriciousness: at fifty yards it could be aimed with some hope of success; up to 200 yards it could be usefully fired at a group, the man actually aimed at being almost certain to escape harm; but over 200 yards, although the ball could carry up to 700, its behaviour was so eccentric that the noise of the discharge was more likely to excite terror than the ball. Rates of fire depended on how thoroughly the soldier performed his loading drills and the care that he took when he aimed. He could fire up to five rounds a minute if he was satisfied with producing an imposing number of bangs without worrying overmuch what happened to his ball. Taking into account battle conditions, a well-trained soldier should have been capable of firing nearly three effective rounds a minute.

Owing to the relative inaccuracy of the musket, the high number of misfires, and also the moral effect of a sudden blast of fire, a volley from a number of men was likely to produce a more awe-inspiring result than a comparable number of single shots, and the more concentrated the fire the more devastating it was likely to be; hence, throughout most of the eighteenth century, soldiers stood shoulder to shoulder in a line that was three ranks deep; the French experimented with four but found that the fire of the fourth was more likely to endanger their comrades than the enemy. At this time the three-deep line was still the normal practice on the Continent as it gave the line a certain solidarity and catered for the replacement of casualties.

The Baker Rifle

In 1800 a committee of field officers met at Woolwich to select a rifle for use by the new Rifle Corps, later to be the Rifle Brigade. The committee examined samples of rifles from Europe and America but eventually settled for one made by Ezekiel Baker, a London gunmaker. The 'Baker Rifle' as it came to be known had a thirty-inch barrel, rifled to a quarter turn with seven grooves; the bore was 0·625 in. The ball ammunition weighed twenty to the pound and the weight of the weapon itself was $9\frac{1}{2}$ lb. Its maximum range was 300 yards and it was extremely accurate up to distances of 200 yards. A triangular sword bayonet, measuring seventeen inches, was fitted.

During the War of American Independence, especially in wild country against irregular bodies of riflemen, the British Army had become accustomed to a looser order. Battalions frequently fought in only two ranks and, by European standards, these were not properly closed up. This was beneficial in that it led Wellington to adopt a two-rank line in the Peninsula, but with the loose order regiments had come to devise tactical manoeuvres of their own and drill had become sloppy and haphazard; the results in Flanders had not always been happy. In 1792 the Duke of York, the Commander-in-Chief, decided that a common tactical doctrine must be adopted by the whole of the infantry and issued a manual entitled *Rules and regulations for the field formation exercise of movements of His Majesty's Forces*, which he proceeded rigorously to enforce. The manual, written by Sir David Dundas, was largely based on formations current in the Prussian Army and has been reviled as intolerably rigid in outlook; nevertheless it gave a sound tactical doctrine to the infantry and was the basis of the battle-drills used in the Peninsula.

Dundas envisaged the men in a battalion standing shoulder to shoulder in a line three ranks deep. (As already mentioned, Wellington reduced this to two.) The first part of his manual was devoted to the individual drills such as turning, marching, and wheeling, that the soldier had to master before he was fit to take his place in his company. In the remainder he laid down a series of drills which, while retaining the rigid, slow-moving line as the battle formation, yet enabled a battalion when not actually engaged in combat to move swiftly and easily over the battlefield. He divided the battalion into eight equal divisions; these roughly corresponded to the eight line companies if the grenadier and light companies were both excluded; if they were present he allowed the number of divisions to be increased to ten; on the other hand, if the battalion was weak the number could be reduced proportionately. In practice it was rare for the light company to form part of the battle-line; its normal task was to screen the front or flanks of the battalion or brigade. The grenadier company, no longer specifically armed with grenades, was composed of the steadiest soldiers in the unit; it might be used for some particularly dangerous task, but the habit of brigading the grenadier companies to make up *ad hoc* grenadier battalions had largely disappeared. In some regiments the grenadier company was divided, half being placed on the right and half on the left of the line. Dundas does not seem to have thought that any specific provision was necessary for its deployment.

Although he described some eighteen manoeuvres in detail, his drills in essence were based on four key formations – column of route, column of divisions, line, and square. Column of route was used for all movement when there was no immediate threat of contact with the enemy. Dundas laid down that this could be carried out in fours if the line formed two deep, sixes if three deep. Since marching men required double the space occupied by the men when stationary the length of a column of route should equal the frontage of the same unit in line, and he emphasized that this length should not be exceeded. March discipline much resembled that in force in the British Army until the 1930s, when the threat from the air enforced a greater degree of dispersion. Battalions started off from their camping-grounds with arms at the slope or shoulder and bands playing. After a short distance the men marched at ease and were permitted to break step. At every hour of the clock there was a short halt to enable the men to rest and adjust their equipment. Before the hourly halt and immediately after it, men marched to attention and in step for a few minutes, and the same drill was observed when they arrived at their destination or were called upon to execute a manoeuvre.

When contact with the enemy became a possibility, column of route was changed to column of divisions, or if the company organization had been preserved, column of companies. In this formation each division deployed in a two-deep line with the divisions ranged one behind the other, No. 1 Division leading; occasionally it might be convenient to have No. 8 in front. Here two rather confusing terms were apt to be used. If No. 1 led, the battalion was said to be 'right in front' if No. 8 'left in front', the terms referring to their respective positions when in line. In some circumstances it was desirable to adopt a compromise between column and line. For this purpose Dundas had enacted that, besides being divided into eight divisions, the battalion line should also be divided into four grand divisions, and column of grand divisions, generally formed by grouping divisions in pairs, might be substituted for column of divisions.

Intervals might be varied. In close column there might be only seven paces between the rear rank of one division and the front rank of the one immediately behind it. On the move, open column was more usual; in this formation the distance between divisions was equal to their front for an important reason: with these intervals the battalion could form line facing left or right very quickly indeed, as each division needed to do no more than execute a separate right or left wheel for the whole to be in line. This was the manoeuvre so brilliantly executed by Pakenham and the 3rd Division at the battle of Salamanca. Forming line to the front was a slower process. Each division came up in succession on the right or left of the division in front of it, depending on the flank ordered, until the line had been formed, while the leading division normally halted to allow the others to catch up; the rear division might therefore find it had some 200 yards to cover, and if, as sometimes happened, the whole brigade was advancing in column of companies or divisions, this distance might be tripled.

Once in line, the colours took post in the centre with the colonel, mounted, six paces behind. The senior major and the adjutant, also mounted, took post respectively behind the 3rd and 6th Divisions; the company commanders, dismounted, took up a position on the right of the front rank of their company or division with a sergeant covering them in the rear rank. The remaining officers and sergeants, the drummers, pioneers, and any other hangers-on formed a third supernumerary rank with orders, as Dundas phrased it, to 'keep the others closed up to the front during the attack and prevent any break beginning in the rear'. The second-in-command of the left-hand division, however, covered by a sergeant, took post on the left flank of that division.

When advancing in line the men on the flanks kept their alignment by dressing on the colours in the centre. If a brigade advanced in line it was the duty of the colour parties to align themselves on the colours of the particular battalion that had been detailed to set pace and direction. In this formation the senior battalion was on the right, the next senior on the left, and the junior in the centre.

The last formation, that of square, Dundas shows as being formed from line. With No. 1 Division on the right and No. 8 on the left, the procedure was as follows. The 4th and 5th Divisions stood fast, the 2nd and 3rd wheeled to their right rear forming a line at right angles to the right flank of No. 4 Division, while the 6th and 7th in a similar manner wheeled to their left rear forming a line at right angles to the left flank of No. 5 Division. The 1st and 8th Divisions closed the square and faced the rear; the officers and colours took post in its centre, the officers waving their swords exultantly in the air whenever a volley was fired.

There were many other drills for forming a square; sometimes it was formed in two ranks, sometimes in four; on occasion two battalions might unite, as at Waterloo, to make up a single square. When two or more squares were necessary, alternate ones would be echelonned back, so that the fire from one could sweep the face of the next. It is evident that if a square were to be formed quickly and without confusion, companies had to be of equal strength, and that some system, such as that of divisions, was probably

The Portuguese were highly competent light infantry, excelling in skirmishing roles. This one is wearing the normal brown uniform and the colour of the facings shows his unit (the 5th Caçadores). (Roffe/Osprey)

This colour-sergeant in the 11th Foot was the equivalent of the modern company sergeant-major, although the rank equivalent is now a stage lower. He wears one chevron below a crown and the Union flag. He carries a short pike and a sword. (Roffe/Osprey)

*This private in the 10th Hussars has a resplendent but practical
uniform. His fur cap kept him warm, and the pelisse round his
shoulders helped to keep the rain out of his neck. His trousers are
leather.* (Roffe/Osprey)

unavoidable. Nevertheless, the advantages of the fighting and the administrative units being identical, so that officers and NCOs knew the men they led in action, became more and more apparent; and the custom of using the company as the tactical unit became steadily more widespread as the war progressed.

To give still greater flexibility in manoeuvre, Dundas decreed that a division should be divided into two sub-divisions and four sections, but added that a section should never number less than five files (fifteen men if the ranks were three deep); these would operate the same formations within a division as a division within a battalion. As the division was the smallest sub-unit under an officer it may be surmised that these smaller formations were rarely used, unless a company was operating independently on its own.

As regards frontages, Dundas stated that a man should occupy twenty-two inches. Two feet, however, would seem a more realistic figure, besides being easier to use for purposes of calculation. A battalion 700 strong, after subtracting the light company, the musicians, and those in the supernumerary third rank, would probably muster about 560 men actually in the battle-line; assuming a front rank of 280, the frontage for such a battalion would be in the region of 200 yards. Such a brigade normally fought with all three battalions in line. Its front would extend about 600 yards. Infantry divisions on the other hand seldom had all three brigades in line. At the Battle of Salamanca the 4th Division did so with disastrous results; Wellington had, however, with customary prescience placed the 6th Division behind it to give the attack depth, and Lowry Cole commanding the 4th may well have taken this into account when determining his formation.

When the manoeuvring had ended and the fighting had begun it was important that at no time should a battalion be discovered with all its muskets unloaded; if this should happen it would be helpless before cavalry, and enemy infantry would be able to close and blast it off the battlefield with impunity. Dundas frowned on file firing whereby each front rank and rear rank man fired immediately after the man on his right, and favoured the firing of volleys. He stated: 'Line will fire by platoons, each battalion independent, and firing beginning from the centre of each.' In his regulations Dundas uses the terms of platoon and company as though they were the same, and presumably meant here that firing would be by company or division; since there was only one officer in the front rank of each division, except for the left flank one, it seems logical to suppose that these were the units of fire; on the other hand it is likely that battalions developed procedures of their own. After the first volley men almost certainly fired independently as fast as possible, the initial method of opening fire ensuring that firing remained continuous. At close range this fire could be murderous; after two or three minutes one side would almost certainly begin to fall into disorder, and seeing this the other would probably clinch matters with the bayonet. Captain Sherer describing his action at the Battle of Albuhera gives some idea what the reality must have been like:

'Just as our line had entirely cleared the Spaniards, the smoky shroud of battle was, by the slackening of fire, for one minute blown aside, and gave to our view the French grenadier caps, their arms, and the whole aspect of their frowning masses. It was a momentary, but a grand sight; a heavy atmosphere of smoke again enveloped us, and few objects could be discerned at all, none distinctly. The murderous contest of musketry lasted long. We were the whole time advancing on and shaking the enemy. At the distance of about twenty yards from them we received orders to charge. We ceased firing, cheered and had our bayonets in the charging position. . . . The French infantry broke and fled, abandoning some guns and howitzers about sixty yards from us. . . . To describe my feelings throughout this wild scene with fidelity would be impossible: at intervals a shriek or a groan told me that men were falling about me; but it was not always that the tumult of the contest suffered me to catch these sounds. A constant feeling [i.e. closing] to the centre of our line and the gradual diminution of our front more truly bespoke the havoc of death.'

For a battalion, the sequence of action might be an approach march in column of route, then a halt at an assembly area where the battalion might close up in column of grand divisions, and stand poised ready to swing into action. Here colours would be uncased and primings checked. Then would come the advance in open column, deployment into line, and finally trial by fire.

During the later stages of the advance the light infantry might well have been deployed in front; while capable of taking their place in the battle-line, they generally had other more important functions to perform. They were equipped with a lighter version of the Brown Bess that had a barrel only thirty-nine inches long. They always acted in pairs – from the time he joined this unit each man had to choose a comrade from whom he was separated neither in camp nor on the battlefield. When a light infantry company operated on its own a few men would be kept in close order as a reserve immediately under the hand of the commander, the rest would be spread in pairs across the front, one member of each a little in front of his comrade so that they could cover each other either in advancing or retiring; the intervals between pairs would vary from two to twelve paces depending on the extent of the front they had to cover. These skirmishers, as they were called, preserved only the roughest of lines, selecting individual firing positions where the best cover could be obtained. Being widely separated, they worked to bugle-calls like the cavalry, not to the drums of the line. In an advance they would close with the enemy's line and while themselves presenting an insignificant target, gall it unmercifully with their fire. In defence they had to present an impenetrable front to the light troops of the enemy; but, once attacked in force, their task was done and they were permitted to withdraw to a flank, taking the utmost care not to mask the fire of their own line as they went. Light companies might work independently, but more often those in a brigade were grouped together under a single commander to form a small light infantry unit, and in the Portuguese brigade all the light companies were already concentrated in the Caçadore battalion.

The Riflemen

In front of the light infantry the riflemen, the élite of the skirmishers, might be seen weaving their way forward. Initially Wellington had three rifle battalions, the 95th, the 5th/60th Rifles, and the Brunswick-Oels Jägers. Later these were increased by the arrival of two more battalions of the 95th, and in addition a number of rifles were made available to the Light Battalions of the King's German Legion. (Sir Charles Oman, in 'History of the Peninsula War', vol. v, *Wellington's Army*) has stated that the Caçadore battalions were armed with rifles and a number of

authorities agree with him. However, taking into account the total production of the Baker Rifle in the United Kingdom, the contention is open to doubt. Possibly some Caçadore battalions were so armed.)

Wellington always allotted at least one company of riflemen to each infantry division; they operated ahead of everyone, slinking from cover to cover like hunters or poachers, rather than the brightly-hued soldiers of the day, and they were the first troops to wear an elementary form of camouflage clothing. The 60th having been raised as the Royal American Regiment wore green to match the forests where they had originated and the 95th did the same; the Brunswick-Oels Jägers wore black, but this was partially to mourn for the rape of Brunswick by Napoleon, while the Caçadores, when not clothed by the British in rifle green, wore brown, perhaps the earliest use of a version of khaki.

Wellington looked to his infantry for his victories, and indeed initially, with few guns and less cavalry, he was given little choice. Perhaps in consequence, although in two of his greatest battles, those of Vitoria and Salamanca, he was the attacker, he won his greatest renown as the master of defence. When selecting his position for a defensive battle he selected a ridge, wherever possible, deploying his troops below its crest and out of sight of the enemy. French commanders encountering such a position rarely saw more than a few scattered guns and, dotting the forward slopes, small groups of light infantry, who discouraged close reconnaissance by accurate fire at remarkably long ranges. When the French came to launch their attack, their massed artillery, unable to see a true target, would be largely ineffective, while their skirmishers would fail to dislodge Wellington's light infantry; then, when their heavy columns, groping their way uncertainly up the ridge through a swarm of skirmishers, finally reached the crest they would suddenly find in front of them a long steady wall of infantry and their leading files would be blown away before they had recovered from their surprise. Even as late as the closing stages of the Battle of Waterloo, Napoleon's Imperial Guard thought they had broken through the British line only to see the Foot Guards emerge out of a cornfield, and drastically enlighten them. It is probable that infantry have never been handled with greater skill than under Wellington and equally that no general was better served by his infantry soldiers.

This officer in the Light Dragoons spent most of his time in patrolling and reconnaissance. His hat was less practical than his other garments and was almost ceremonial. (Roffe/Osprey)

This private in the 3rd Dragoon Guards – heavy cavalry – wears a heavy coatee, heavy gauntlets, and carries a metal helmet with brass chin-scales to protect the throat. (Roffe/Osprey)

The Cavalry

Paradoxically enough, the basic organization of a cavalry regiment bore a marked similarity to that of an infantry battalion. It was commanded by a lieutenant-colonel with two majors, ten captains, and twenty lieutenants or cornets under him; it consisted of ten troops, each under a captain, and had a war establishment of about eighty privates (the term trooper was not then used) and eighty horses. From time to time there were minor variations in the numbers, but substantially these figures held good for the whole period of the war.

The number of men actually present with the regiment, especially after a long period in the field, was considerably less. In *Rules and regulations for the cavalry, 1796* for instance, it was directed that: 'Each troop should be divided into two squads when under forty, into three or more when above, according to the number, with an equal number of non-commissioned officers in each. . . . The squads must be as separate and distinct as possible. . . . The squad is entirely in the charge of its own sergeant.' This seems to have relieved the junior officers of all administrative responsibilities. However, they were ordered to 'look in on the men at dinner hours', regrettably not so much to check the quality of the rations as to see that

Le Marchant's heavy brigade making the vital charge at Salamanca which broke the French infantry. This battle is described as 'Wellington's masterpiece'.

their men 'do not dispose of their meat for liquor'. In an optimistic vein the Regulations continued: 'nor is any dragoon to give way to that blackguard practice of swearing'. Officers too, had to preserve a certain decorum and the Regulations emphasized: 'on no account is an officer to wear his hat on the back of his head'.

In some minor ways the cavalry organization took into account the differences of that arm from the infantry. The senior non-commissioned officer in a troop was the troop-quartermaster and in regimental headquarters there was a riding-master with rough riders under him to train horses and men. As in the infantry there was an adjutant and a sergeant-major; the latter's duties included drilling the young officers and these had to pay him a guinea and a half for the privilege of listening to his words of counsel couched, no doubt, in traditional terms.

Cavalry regiments fell into two main categories, heavy and light. The distinction at this time had little significance so far as their duties in the field were concerned. Heavy cavalry might find themselves on

outpost duty, as did Le Marchant's Heavy Cavalry Brigade during the siege of Ciudad Rodrigo, while the Light might execute a fierce charge as they did at the cavalry combat at Villa-Garcia. The heavy cavalry tended to be larger men on larger horses and to carry heavier weapons, but, unlike the French

Firing from the saddle was difficult enough under any conditions but particularly so when the horse reared with alarm.

cuirassiers, they wore no body armour; in theory they were better suited for shock action on the field of battle, while the nimbler and more agile light horsemen might be expected to excel at outpost duty, patrolling, and the pursuit. Wellington himself paid little attention to such niceties, using regiments as convenient without much regard to their official classification.

The heavy cavalrymen went into action with a cut-down version of the Brown Bess musket, labelled a carbine, which had a barrel twenty-six inches long. His main weapon was a long, heavy, badly-balanced sword, according to some critics the worst weapon ever issued to the British Army. The light cavalryman was also armed with a carbine, the Paget, which had an exceptionally short barrel, only sixteen inches, but again his main weapon was his sabre, about thirty-three inches long and reputedly a light and handy weapon. Officers carried a similar pattern sword to that of their men, and all ranks carried pistols. It was in their uniforms that the two types of cavalrymen differed most distinctly. Historically, the regular cavalry had developed from regiments of dragoons and in origin the dragoon had been little more than an infantryman on horseback. Marlborough, however, believed in shock action and the sword, limiting his cavalrymen to no more than three or four rounds for their carbines in battle, and this view had become generally accepted. The heavy cavalry regiments, still called dragoons or, more grandiosely, dragoon guards, however, retained in their uniform their old infantry connexion, and at the beginning of the war were attired in red coats and white breeches. The light cavalry, light dragoons or, more rarely, hussars, by now had totally renounced their origin. The colour of their jackets was basically blue, but became so adorned with wonderful and exotic additions that the modern Paris fashions would have had little to offer the well-dressed light dragoon.

But here the differences largely ended; neither in drills nor in composition does there appear to have been any great distinction. However, a marked difference soon developed between cavalry and infantry. Cavalry regiments had no battalions or depots, and were responsible for recruiting and training their own men; in addition, with their imposing chargers and cutting swords that could wound but seldom kill, they were far better at controlling riotous mobs than the infantry with their

deadlier firearms and vicious bayonets that could be used only for the far more lethal thrust. Since the free-born Briton of the day was accustomed to voicing his views with no little force, the government made a habit of keeping a number of cavalry regiments in the country to help enforce its less popular decrees. For these reasons, cavalry regiments serving in the Peninsula normally left behind two troops to form a depot, going overseas with only eight, and later some regiments left behind four.

When the 10th Royal Hussars left England to join Wellington for his campaign of 1813, four troops under a major were sent to York to form a depot and keep an eye on the local populace, while according to its official history the regiment embarked six troops strong, with the following: lieutenant-colonels, 1; majors, 1; staff officers, 4 (presumably these were officers in regimental headquarters and included the adjutant, the quartermaster, and perhaps a doctor and veterinary surgeon); captains, 6; subalterns, 12; assistant adjutant, 1; regimental sergeant-major, 1; troop quartermaster, 2; troop sergeant-majors, 4; sergeants, 29; corporals, 24; trumpeters, 6; privates, 513; troop horses, 523. It is interesting to note that troop sergeant-majors appear to have begun to take over from troop-quartermasters.

Although the regiment had only six troops, with about 580 rank and file, it was considerably stronger than many of the eight-troop regiments serving in the Peninsula at this time. Here the strength of most regiments fluctuated between 400 and 500; a number were considerably less. Yet in 1809 some of the cavalry regiments serving under Sir John Moore had mustered as many as 750 men. Even allowing for the wastage to be expected in service, it seems clear that the smaller regiments had proved more effective in the field.

On operations, no doubt for what must have appeared at that time good reason, the troop organization was almost entirely abandoned; troops worked in pairs to form squadrons under the senior troop commanders, and, curiously, the half-squadron, not the troop, was the basic sub-unit for manoeuvre. Captain Neville, in his treatise on light cavalry which was largely embodied in the cavalry manual of 1803, put forward the view that thirty-six or forty-eight files (i.e. seventy-two or ninety-six men and horses) composed a manageable squadron. This suggests that an eight-troop regiment organized in four squadrons was at its best with under 400 men present in the ranks.

To adopt the operational organization, troops first paraded and sized; then each pair of troops came together to form a squadron in a two-rank line with the largest men from both in the centre; when in line the men on the flanks tended to lean inwards setting up a considerable pressure on the centre, and for this reason the heaviest men were placed there to prevent their being forced out of the ranks like corks from bottles of champagne. It seems unlikely that during operations this clumsy procedure was always followed, and in an emergency squadrons must surely have fallen in as such.

The intervals to be observed within the squadron were carefully defined. Between the front and rear ranks there was to be a horse's length; men in close order rode with their boot-tops touching; in loose files boot-tops were to be six inches apart; and in open files there was an interval of a horse's length between every man. When the squadron had been formed and the men had checked their dressing on the centre file, they were numbered and detailed into half-squadrons, quarter-squadrons, and threes (as in the infantry the nomenclature was somewhat haphazard and such phrases as divisions and sub-divisions were occasionally used).

The numbering in threes was important. The space taken by a horse in the ranks was reckoned at three feet, or a third of a horse's length. Hence if every three men in a rank wheeled their horses independently to the right, the rank would face in that direction in column of threes with a horse's length between each three. It would then be in a very manageable formation, and, when it had reached its new position, on the command 'front' the men could wheel to the left and, since there was a horse's length between each three, could resume line without falling into disorder. In a squadron both ranks would perform this manoeuvre simultaneously, the rear rank wheeling up besides their opposite numbers in the front rank and the whole squadron facing to the right or left in a column of sixes. (The drill was in practice a little more complex than that outlined here, as it involved men reining back.) Movement by threes was normally used for all changes of formation. In true British style, when the order 'threes about' was given, in fact the squadron moved on a front of six men.

For movement over any distance, it was recommended that regiments should move in column of half-squadrons, or if this was impossible, by threes (i.e. sixes) or as a last resort in file or single file. The principle was that wherever feasible the length of the regimental column should not exceed that of the regiment in line.

As in the infantry, the main battle formations were columns of half-squadrons or squadrons, and line. In line, owing to the peril of pressure developing on the centre, an interval was preserved between squadrons, and in an advance the men in each aligned themselves on the centre file of their own particular squadron; the squadron leader himself rode a horse's length in front of his centre man and therefore could control the pace and direction of the whole squadron. To ensure that the regiment preserved its line the squadron leaders of the flank squadrons aligned themselves on those in the centre, while these in turn took their positions from the commanding officer who gallantly rode in the centre of his regiment a horse's length in front of the rank of squadron leaders, a rather more hazardous position than that occupied by the infantry colonel, happily ensconced six paces behind his colours. Of the remaining officers and sergeants in the squadron, an officer covered by a sergeant took post on each of its flanks, three sergeants occupied positions on the right of quarter-squadrons, and the rest made up a serre-file, or supernumerary rank, a horse's length behind the rear rank. The trumpeter or trumpeters rode in the serre-file, but directly behind the squadron leader. Commands were initially given by word of mouth, generally repeated by the appropriate call on the trumpet; the most important calls such as 'charge' or 'rally' were taken up by all the trumpeters. Bugles were sometimes used instead of trumpets, but the manual of 1803 clearly thought this was a deplorable surrender to utility. It stated of the bugle-horn: 'Soundings are exactly the same as those for the trumpet in place of which the bugle-horn may occasionally be substituted. The trumpet is always to be considered as the principal musical instrument for the sounding; it particularly belongs to the line and the bugle-horn to detached parties.'

The main cavalry method of attack was the charge. On this subject the manual of 1803 stated: 'When cavalry attack cavalry, the squadrons must be firm and compact; when they attack infantry the files may be opened; when they attack a battery, they must not

This gunner is in service dress. He is still wearing the pre-1812 stovepipe shako. The red cord carries the powder-flash. His sword bayonet is for personal defence. (Roffe/Osprey)

The Sapper, who belongs to the Royal Sappers and Miners, is wearing the red coatee which replaced blue after 1813. Otherwise the uniform resembles ordinary infantry pattern apart from the white plume and bastion loops. (Roffe/Osprey)

ride up in front of it, but they must in two divisions attack on each flank, the files opened.

'When cavalry attack infantry they should in general do it in column; the squadrons of the column should have at least three times as much distance between them as the extent of their front. The leading squadron, after breaking the enemy's line should move forward and form, the two succeeding ones should wheel outwards by half squadrons and charge along the line.' The action after a charge was important. The manual continues, 'In a charge of either infantry or cavalry the instant the enemy gives way the line must again be formed and the pursuit continued by light troops.' This was easy enough to

lay down, but it was a ruling all too often forgotten in practice. Time and again the British cavalry failed to rally after a successful charge, galloping off in a wild pursuit of their beaten enemy, only to be confronted, when horses were blown, by fresh French cavalry and their triumph to be turned into disaster.

In a charge against infantry, the gallop began about 300 yards away to cut to a minimum the time under fire; against cavalry, on the other hand, the most important consideration was to arrive with reasonably fresh horses for the mêlée, and only the last 150 yards were covered at a gallop. It is difficult to believe that two squadrons ever galloped at each other in a compact mass. If they did so they would

Manual Exercise according to the late regulation by the Duke of York.
See Treatise on Military Affairs.

1 Prime & Load   2 Handle Cartridge   3 Prime

4 Load   5 Draw Ramrod   6 Ram down Cartridge

The complicated and lengthy process of loading and firing is shown in this extract from a manual of musketry exercises.

have resembled two motorists driving along the crown of the road and colliding with a closing speed of thirty miles an hour, and the drivers would have been in a much happier position than the cavalryman on his horse. Lieutenant-Colonel W. Tomkinson, who served throughout the Peninsular War in the 16th Light Dragoons, made some illuminating comments, in *Diary of a Cavalry Officer*, when describing a skirmish:

'Captain Belli's squadron with one of the Hussars, was in advance; and the enemy having sent forward two or three squadrons, Major Myers attempted to oppose them in front of a defile. He waited so long and was so indecisive, and the enemy coming up so close, that he ordered the squadron of the 16th to charge. The enemy's squadron was about twice their strength and waited their charge.

'This is the first instance I ever met with two bodies of cavalry coming into opposition, and both standing, as invariably as I have observed it, one or the other runs away.

'Our men rode up and began sabring, but were so outnumbered that they could do nothing and were obliged to retire across the defile in confusion, the enemy having brought up more troops to that point.'

The ability to outflank an enemy was clearly one of the keys to a successful cavalry action and the length of front was of critical importance. The manual specified: 'Two or three squadrons in attack may divide into small bodies with 14 or 16 files in each and intervals between them equal to their front, the second or reserve covering the intervals 150 yards to the rear; if only two squadrons, the first line should be four small troops, the second of two again sub-divided, three covering the intervals and one outflanking.' The use of the word 'troop' here illustrates the remarkably casual attitude to terminology typical of the period.

In the rugged country of the Portuguese border

The Drum Major wears a distinctive yellow coat which enabled him to be picked out quickly in battle when special calls might need to be sounded. (Roffe/Osprey)

The Duke of Wellington. His military genius lay not merely in strategy and tactics but in the creation of an army which knew it would win.

and of much of Spain, the cavalry had few opportunities to exert a decisive influence in battle. Their most valuable functions were to act as the eyes and ears of the army and to screen it in movement and at rest. Single well-mounted sentries called *vedettes* could observe and hang around an enemy and gallop away if threatened. The tactics of the cavalry when patrolling or on outpost were strikingly similar to those of the light infantry. They worked in pairs in open order, covering each other and using their carbines to fire from the saddle – apart from the difficulty of persuading their horses to stand still while aiming and firing, reloading must have presented nearly insuperable problems and one suspects that the effect of such fire was moral rather than physical.

The standard cavalry formation was the brigade composed of two, three or, less usually, four regiments. During the early stages of the war Wellington formed two cavalry divisions; although these on occasion consisted of two brigades, one heavy, one light, their organization was far more fluid than that of the infantry and tended to reflect the needs of a particular situation. He was plagued by incompetent divisional commanders, and from 1812 onwards discarded the division organization, leaving the cavalry brigades largely independent under the general direction of a single cavalry commander, General Sir Stapleton Cotton, who normally exercised control from army headquarters.

For most of the war Wellington was heavily outnumbered in cavalry by the French. During the first three years he had only eight regiments, but towards the end of 1811 matters improved. During the Salamanca campaign of 1812 he had sixteen, and used his new-found strength to decisive advantage at the Battle of Salamanca. Here Le Marchant, with a

General Lord Hill, 'Daddy Hill', Wellington's most trusted subordinate commander.

Heavy Cavalry Brigade, in brilliant charge shattered a tottering French line to turn a French reverse into utter defeat.

The following year at Vitoria and during the battles in the Pyrenees the country inhibited the use of large bodies of horsemen. However, during Wellington's great advance through Spain to the borders of France the cavalry faithfully imposed an impenetrable screen in front of his armies and enabled him utterly to deceive the French commanders.

The Artillery

The organization of the Royal Artillery reflected the somewhat casual fashion in which that arm had evolved; it had a logic all its own. Gunners were men who fired guns; guns were tubes down which various types of projectiles could be stuffed to be subsequently blown to a remote destination. The process clearly required certain specialized skills not to be found in the infantry, but, since one tube, give or take a few feet in length and a few inches in diameter, much resembled another, a man who could deal with one manifestly could deal with another. It would be a false and expensive move, therefore, to train gunners to deal with only one particular type of equipment; what was needed was a number of all-purpose gunners capable of firing any type of cannon that might be appropriate to the task of the moment.

At the beginning of the eighteenth century, when it had become clear that artillery was likely to be a permanent feature of the battlefield, the British Army raised a Royal Regiment of Artillery consisting of a single battalion. The old Roman organization of tens and centuries which seemed to work well enough for the infantry was obviously equally suitable for gunners. When, over the years, more battalions were raised they were composed of ten companies each about a hundred strong. These companies were expected to man any type of cannon, so there seemed little point in issuing them with a standard number of guns, or indeed any guns at all. When the need arose a battery of guns could be drawn from the gun-park, the number and type being those deemed suitable for the particular task. Since it might prove unnecessary to move the guns it would be folly to provide any form of transport. The infantry humped their muskets, there seemed no reason why the gunners should not pull their guns; if transport should be necessary, the sensible answer was to hire contractors for the occasion and discharge them when the occasion was over.

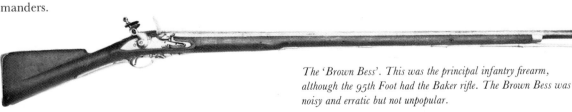

The 'Brown Bess'. This was the principal infantry firearm, although the 95th Foot had the Baker rifle. The Brown Bess was noisy and erratic but not unpopular.

39

This Royal Engineers officer is wearing a cocked hat which shows he is in a specialist all-officer corps. Neither Engineer nor Artillery commissions could be purchased but were allotted to cadets who came highest in the order of merit at the Royal Military Academy. (Roffe/Osprey)

A Pioneer, as shown here, worked with the Infantry in clearing obstacles. In addition to a rifle and a sword-bayonet he carried a felling axe. Note the leather apron. (Roffe/Osprey)

It was a delightfully simple approach and one likely to appeal strongly to those in financial authority. The possibility that, while it might provide the cheapest form of artillery, the system was hardly likely to produce the most efficient, was only slowly and reluctantly accepted. The first reform came when some astute member of the Board of Ordnance, which controlled such matters, realized that invalid companies were quite fit enough to man the guns on permanent fortifications, and thus the first tentative

attempt at specialization was introduced. This reform, being an economy, was relatively painless. But the next, the decision to discontinue the hiring of civilian contractors to transport guns, was another matter. Yet civilian transport had indisputable disadvantages. Civilians, for some inscrutable reason of their own, were very apt to depart from the battlefield at the most critical moments, leaving the guns stranded or without ammunition. As these civilians were not subject to military law, the only

*The 95th (the Rifle Brigade) in action with their Baker rifles.
Here they are covering the right flank of their advancing infantry.*

punishment was to discharge them, a service that they had frequently already performed for themselves. By the time of the Peninsular War, however, a Corps of Royal Artillery Drivers had been raised, but this corps was completely separate from the Royal Regiment of Artillery and was commanded by officers from the Commissary. It was organized in troops from which drivers and horses were allotted to the artillery companies as might be necessary. This was the organization in force in the Peninsula. When a company of artillery had been allotted a battery of guns and the wherewithal to move them, it was known as a 'Brigade of Artillery'. This term, which had a completely different significance for most of the first half of this century, may be confusing; since these brigades corresponded to what in modern parlance would be called a field battery, it will, perhaps, be less confusing to use this title.

In the early days of the Peninsular War the finding of the gunners from one source and transport and guns from others had the unfortunate results to be expected; in particular the gunners tended to suffer from a critical shortage of transport. However, with the passage of time the artillery companies operated for long periods with a particular type of gun and a roughly standardized amount of transport, but even then a company might find itself suddenly drafted to man siege-guns, and the provision of horses and drivers to make the guns mobile still had its problems.

In 1813 Captain Cairns, commanding an artillery company, wrote, as quoted by Sir Alexander Dickson in *The Dickson Manuscripts 1812–13*:

'We, that is our brigade [i.e. battery] and the Household Cavalry, arrived here on the 27th. Although marching with them we are not in their brigade; however, as we are of the Reserve, I am quite well pleased with them, as with no superior officers of our corps being now left to myself to forage and arrange as I please.

'I am getting my naked drivers clothed here as well as I can. These lads were only three days in Lisbon, when they were pushed up to the Army and unluckily fell to my lot.

The Battle of Castalla depicted here shows a British Infantry battalion facing an attack by French Infantry in column. Note the company officers on the flanks of their companies.

'They leave England paid in advance, sell half their necessaries when lying at Portsmouth and the other half either at Lisbon or on the road, the driver officers never inspecting their kit. Thus they join a brigade perfectly naked. In my establishment of 100 drivers, I have men from three different Troops. I am resolved to see that my officer of drivers, Lieutenant Dalton, does his duty in supplying them with necessaries, soap and salt. That is all I allow him to interfere with. My own officers look to the stable duties, and inspect the drivers' kits of their division every Saturday. The poor drivers are sadly to be pitied – considering the labour of taking care of two horses and harness they are worse paid than any other troops, and when left to the management of their own officers they are luckless indeed. By being with a brigade there is some hope of instilling into them the idea that they are soldiers.'

Marshal Beresford, an exceptionally strong man, dealing with a Polish lancer at Albuhera.

British Hussars charging French cavalry. Note there are no plumes in the headdress, but these hussars are all the fortunate possessors of chin-straps.

The first part of this letter indicates another curious aspect of the artillery organization. At any one time an artillery battalion might have its companies spread as far apart as the West Indies, Spain, and Sicily. All attempts to concentrate battalions in particular regions invariably failed and the commanding officers, accepting with philosophy the impossibility of visiting their companies, generally stayed in Woolwich, contenting themselves with organizing drafts and looking after the administration of their companies overseas. In consequence there tended to be no real gunner hierarchy with the armies in the field. In operations near England, such as that at Walcheren, a reasonable number of senior officers might take part, but farther afield there was often only one senior artillery officer, perhaps a major, who acted as the Commander, Royal Artillery, and his duties rarely extended to more than solving the many administrative problems which the peculiar gunner organization was likely to produce.

At this time the Royal Horse Artillery wore a uniform closely akin to that of the Light Dragoons, with numerous loops. This gunner has the artillery colours of blue and red facings and gold lace. On his helmet is the artillery white plume. (Roffe/Osprey)

This Royal Artillery officer has a blue coat signifying that the regiment belonged to the Ordnance. Other units wore red coats. Note the white plume. (Roffe/Osprey)

The artillery company commanders were virtually independent, and as Cairn's letter shows, they were probably far from dissatisfied with their fate.

In the Peninsula the artillery was, first, officially in the charge of a Major-General, Royal Artillery. He seldom accompanied the army in the field, partly because Wellington seems to have taken a dislike to the two generals who successively occupied the post.

During most of the war he took as his artillery adviser Major Alexander Dickson (later Major-General Sir Alexander Dickson) a captain in the Royal Artillery who had transferred to the Portuguese service to obtain a step in rank. It was a fortunate choice, and quite possibly Wellington was happy to have as his artillery adviser an officer too junior to press on him gratuitous advice, something he detested. During the

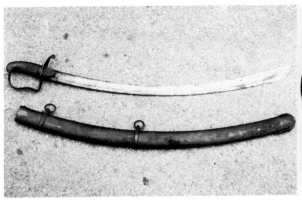

A typical trooper's Light Cavalry pattern sabre, which was, of course, curved. Heavy dragoons carried a straight sword.

A 5½-inch howitzer. Note the short barrel for high-angle firing.

course of the war, Dickson was promoted Lieutenant-Colonel and in 1813 was appointed to command all the artillery in the field. By the time of the Battle of Vitoria he had accumulated the nucleus of a staff, and majors were to be found on occasion co-ordinating the activities of two or more batteries.

This lack of a gunner hierarchy, particularly during the early period, may have influenced Wellington against using his artillery massed. He allotted one battery semi-permanently to each division and that battery rarely strayed far from its parent formation. The reserve artillery was generally

minimal in strength and artillery tactics seldom rose above the level of the battery. At this level the standard became remarkably high.

But although the company of Royal Foot Artillery in the Peninsula remained a maid-of-all-work, the first step in producing a battery trained and equipped for the field had already been taken. On 1 January 1793 orders were issued for the formation of A and B Troops, Royal Horse Artillery. These Troops were designed to act with the cavalry, and, therefore, had to be highly mobile, fast into action, and quick and accurate in their shooting. They were trained almost

Royal Artillery Drivers. They wore the same pattern helmet as the Royal Horse Artillery.

exclusively in their own particular role, and their drivers, although initially drawn from the Corps of Royal Artillery Drivers, were carried on the Troop strength and to all intents and purposes formed an integral part of the unit. Only officers of proven ability and the pick of the recruits were posted in. As a result these troops soon established a very high reputation. Since they supported the cavalry, they adopted a light cavalry style of uniform quite different from that of their comrades with the infantry. Troops of R.H.A. supported the two cavalry divisions in the Peninsula and that most famous of divisions, the Light Division.

In an embarkation return dated 8 June 1809 quoted in Captain Duncan's *History of the Royal Artillery*, Captain Ross's Troop, R.H.A. is shown as being composed as follows:

Captains		2
Subalterns		3
Assistant Surgeons		1
NCOs		13
Trumpeters		1
Artificers		7
Gunners		81
Drivers		54
	Total	162
Horses		162
6-pounder guns		5
$5\frac{1}{2}$ in. howitzers		1
Ammunition wagons		6
Baggage wagons		3

This shows a troop of R.H.A. at full strength. Whether horse or field, batteries were commanded by captains with 'second captains' to understudy them. The light six-pounders and the howitzer were generally drawn by teams of six horses, but, for the wagons, mules might be substituted. Gunners carried sabres but the drivers were unarmed. During the campaigns the R.H.A. fully justified their position as the right of the line, and at the Battle of Fuentes d'Onoro under Captain Ramsay, their second captain, Bull's Troop, R.H.A. performed a famous feat. The Troop was cut off by French cavalry and was given up for lost by the remainder of the army. Ramsay, however, limbered up his guns and charged the French cavalry at the gallop. The gunners broke through the astonished French horsemen and re-joined the Army with their guns intact.

The work of the Companies of Royal Foot Artillery, although less glamorous, was no less vital to the success of British arms. Since their guns were heavier than those of the horse artillery, these companies had rather more gunners on establishment. In the Dickson papers a company was shown with an authorized establishment of two captains, three subalterns, four sergeants, four corporals, nine bombardiers, 120 gunners, and three drummers, giving a total of 145 all ranks. In the field, its strength probably fluctuated between 110 and 130. The battery was armed with five field guns, 9-pounders or heavy 6-pounders, and one $5\frac{1}{2}$-inch howitzer. In addition it might have allotted to it about 100 drivers and horses and mules totalling altogether nearly 200. Teams of eight horses harnessed in pairs were normally used to drag the guns, but for the ammunition and baggage (a standard field battery might have eight ammunition and three baggage wagons plus a travelling forge) mules were often employed. However, the companies were far from standardized and would reflect in their organization the prejudices of their company commanders, or the needs of a particular task. The drivers would have a commissary officer theoretically in charge of them, and being mounted, and therefore unable to understand drum-calls, had their own trumpeter.

The characteristics of the guns in both field batteries and the Horse Artillery troops differed little, those in the horse artillery being merely lighter for greater speed of movement. There were three main types of projectile: roundshot, grape, and shell. Roundshot was a solid iron ball that had an extreme effective range of about 1,200 yards. It depended for its effect on the velocity with which it struck its target, hence field guns needed long, heavy barrels to stand up to large charges and impart a high muzzle velocity. On the other hand, since these barrels had to be mounted on robust yet light carriages that could travel across country unharmed and at a reasonable speed, the weight of the barrel had to be severely limited; British field pieces initially only took a 6 lb. ball, not a very daunting missile, and later a model was introduced capable of firing one of 9 lb.

Roundshot, unless striking a column of troops, was comparatively harmless, but it was the only missile that could be used against a moving target at ranges of over 300 yards. Under this distance grape was far more effective. This name was applied in-

The Royal Artillery officer is personally laying the siege gun; two others are noting where the shots fall. The man with the handspike is a bombardier.

discriminately to grapeshot itself, canister, and case. Grapeshot consisted of about nine iron balls sewn together in a canvas bag that dissolved after the rounds left the gun, and received its title from its resemblance to an over-size bunch of grapes; it was issued only to the 18-pounder and 24-pounder guns of the siege train. Case and canister, as the names imply, were metal containers filled with a hundred small bullets or forty large ones. The container disintegrated as the round left the muzzle and the shot fanned out to produce a deadly pattern of destruction for a distance of nearly 300 yards.

Between 300 and 1,000 yards, shells could be very effective, but only if the target was reasonably stationary. The common shell, as it was called, consisted of a hollow iron ball containing a fuse and a bursting charge. The fuse was ignited by the explosion of the charge that propelled the shell, and if all went well, it would cause the bursting charge to explode after the shell had landed; fragments of the exploding shell-case would, it was hoped, strike

anyone rash enough to be standing nearby. To achieve this desirable result it was necessary that the shell should have thin walls and carry a large bursting charge, so that the casing broke up into numerous fragments moving with a lethal velocity; in consequence the shell was too large and too fragile to be fired from a field gun. However, the shell did not need to be given the high muzzle velocity of roundshot and a shorter, lighter piece could be used. The $5\frac{1}{2}$-inch howitzer, the standard field piece for firing shells, although capable of accommodating a 24 lb. ball, owing to its light construction and short barrel (only 33 inches compared with 72 inches for the light 6-pounder, 96 inches for the heavy, and 84 inches for the 9-pounder) could keep up even with the cavalry.

Since field guns could not fire shells, every battery included a howitzer. This complicated the arrangements for ammunition, and experiments were made with all-howitzer batteries, but these proved too specialized to suit the dispersed way in which Wellington generally deployed his guns.

There was an obvious need to make field guns more effective at ranges over 300 yards and Lieutenant Shrapnel developed a shell originally called spherical case, but which later attained more fame under the

47

At the Battle of Fuentes d'Onoro the Royal Horse Artillery are changing ground. In the front of the picture, Wellington, in low cocked hat, is giving orders.

name of its inventor. He filled his shell with bullets; now, as the bursting charge had only to be strong enough to break open the shell case and let loose the bullets, it could be much reduced and the walls of the shell could be thinner. Spherical case was issued to all field guns, although technical difficulties prevented its being fully effective at that time.

In a regimental order the following proportions were laid down for a hundred rounds. Field guns were to carry 60 rounds roundshot, 30 of spherical case and 10 of common case; howitzers, 50 rounds spherical case, 10 rounds common case, and 40 rounds common shell. Ammunition was to be carried at the scale of 180 rounds per 6-pounder gun, 116 per 9-pounder and 84 per howitzer.

In action, guns were aimed by lining up the barrel with the target, hence the gun-layer for either field guns or howitzers had to have a clear view of his target. Range was obtained by elevating the barrel, but even with howitzers it was rare to elevate it more than 10° with the horizontal.

To load the gun, first a charge of gunpowder was rammed down the barrel, then the missile, and finally some wadding to keep it in place. At the same time powder was trickled down a vent which led to the charge, or some combustible material was inserted. When the order to fire was given, a slow match or port-fire was applied to this powder which burnt down to the charge and caused it to explode. Immediately after firing, the gun-barrel had to be sponged out to remove any burning embers that might remain and prematurely ignite the next charge; if for any reason a sponge was not available the gun was out of action. Five or six men were sufficient to load and point a gun but four or five more were needed to prepare the ammunition and help haul it back to its firing position, as the shock of each discharge would cause it to recoil a few feet. Rates of

Artillerymen in Murray's Division crossing the River Douro. The horse on the right seems rather reluctant to enter a boat.

fire are not known for certain. General B. P. Hughes, perhaps the best authority on the subject, calculated that under battle conditions guns could probably fire two rounds of roundshot or three of grape in a minute. Dickson merely observed that the rate of fire for howitzers was slower than that for guns: it may be guessed at about three rounds in two minutes.

Besides the field artillery there were two more categories in the Peninsula, the siege train, which will be considered later, and rockets. Although in the Peninsula no complete battery of rockets ever operated, as Wellington viewed their uncertain behaviour with considerable distaste, it is recorded that 'Captain Lane's rocket detachment did good service during the crossing of the R. Adour before the battle of Orthes[z].' Rockets had been used against the British by the Mahrattas in India in the 1780s as a substitute for artillery. An improved version was

developed at Woolwich by William Congreve in 1805. They consisted of a steel case with a cone or spherical-shaped head, which was usually filled with powder. The largest weighed 24 lbs. Their lack of accuracy made rockets unpopular and they were rarely used between 1840 and World War II.

Wellington's handling of his artillery has sometimes been called in question, yet his method corresponded exactly to his own particular tactical policy. Napoleon concentrated his artillery and signalled his attacks by massive bombardments. Wellington, generally fighting on the defensive, was determined to conceal his dispositions until the last possible moment; he therefore spread his artillery across his front, placing the batteries under the control of his divisional commanders, so that it was possible for the commander on the spot to use his guns to best advantage without the hampering rigidity inevitable under a system of centralized control. Concentrations of artillery might indeed pave the way for a successful attack, but in defence this could

At the siege of Ciudad Rodrigo in 1812 the French tried to break out and capture some breaching batteries. They were unsuccessful.

result in furnishing an easy target for the guns of the enemy and might rob an area of vitally needed artillery support.

At the same time Wellington was quite competent to deploy his individual batteries to best advantage himself. At the Battle of Salamanca the French had a considerable superiority in artillery, but it was the British guns that exercised the most influence on the battle. During the initial attack on the French flank, they were positioned at right angles to the infantry line of advance and raked the front of the French columns with deadly effect. When, later in the battle, Clausel launched a counter-attack that achieved a considerable initial success, the French infantry found themselves advancing up a shallow valley with the British artillery, personally posted by Wellington long before, pouring in a devastating cross-fire from

the high ground on either side, a fire which contributed powerfully to their eventual repulse. It was perhaps natural for the Royal Artillery to watch enviously Napoleon's technique for handling guns *en masse*, a technique perfectly suited to the tactics he used. It did not follow that Wellington's less ostentatious use of that arm was any less well suited to the tactics that at Waterloo led to the defeat of the Emperor of the French.

Sieges and Sappers

The organization of the Royal Artillery may have seemed peculiar, but the organization of the Royal Engineers had the distinction of being barely discernible. For most of the eighteenth century, like the inmates of a college at a university with fellows and dons but no undergraduates, Royal Engineer officers were unencumbered by the presence of soldiers. They moved in the aura of a mysterious craft no lesser mortals could comprehend, and depended

A dramatic picture of the Battle of Fuentes d'Onoro in 1811.

on contract labour for the execution of their designs.

However, after the capture of Gibraltar it was realized that contract labour might not relish repairing fortifications while a siege was actually in progress, and a company of military artificers was raised for this purpose. Later, when revolutionary France threatened invasion, new companies under Engineer officers were formed to fortify the English coastline and the name was changed to the Corps of Royal Military Artificers.

But this corps remained distinct from the Royal Engineers and at the time of the Peninsular War Engineer officers still had virtually no troops under their command; in addition, although they were competent enough in the art of fortification, as they showed when constructing the Lines of Torres Vedras, they had no experience and little knowledge of how to conduct a siege. Since sieges were considered pre-eminently the province of the Engineer assisted by the Artilleryman, being clearly too complicated for the ordinary army officer to understand, the inexperience of the engineers, and above all the lack of trained engineer units was to cost the Peninsular army very dear. The tragedy was the greater in that during the eighteenth century an elaborate ritual had developed by which a siege, if the attackers had sufficient men and siege-guns, became largely a formal and relatively bloodless exercise in excavation and mathematics. General Jones, who as a young engineer officer was present at all Wellington's major sieges, has described the accepted procedure in *Journal of the Sieges in Spain, vol i*: the besiegers broke ground about 700 yards from the ramparts of the fortress:

'This is effected by secretly approaching the place in the night with a body of men carrying entrenching tools and the remainder armed. The former dig a trench in the ground parallel to the fortifications to be attacked, whilst those with arms remain in readiness to protect those at work should the garrison sally out. During the night this trench is made of sufficient extent to cover from the missiles of the place the number of men requisite to cope with the garrison. . . . This trench is afterwards progressively widened and deepened till it forms a covered road called a parallel, and along this road guns, wagons and men can securely move equally sheltered from the view and the missiles of the garrison. Batteries of guns and mortars are then constructed on the side of the road next the garrison and in a short time by superiority of fire silence all those [enemy guns] which bear on the works of the attack.'

The procedure was continued at distances progressively nearer the enemy and, from about 500 yards onwards, heavy guns using roundshot would start to batter a gap, called a breach, in the ramparts of the fortress. While the guns demolished a selected section of the wall the mortars had an important task to perform. They resembled stocky wide-mouthed howitzers with barrels permanently set at an angle of forty-five degrees: their role was to lob large bombs into or over the fixed defences of the enemy, subduing their fire and enabling the construction of the parallels and the covered road to proceed until the covered road led into the breach itself. At this juncture it was customary for the garrison to admit defeat and walk out with the 'honours of war'. If properly carried out, time and gunpowder were consumed rather than lives.

The main difficulty arose when the approaches came within 300 yards of the enemy ramparts. Jones continues:

'Then the work becomes truly hazardous and can only be preformed by selected brave men who have acquired a difficult and most dangerous art called sapping from which they themselves are styled sappers. An indispensable auxiliary to the sapper is the miner, the exercise of whose art requires an even greater degree of skill, courage, and conduct, than that of his principal. The duty of the miner at a siege is to accompany the sapper, to listen for and discover the enemy's miner at work underground, and prevent his blowing up the head of the road either by sinking down and meeting him, when a subterranean conflict ensues, or by running a gallery close to his opponent

and forcing him to quit his work by means of suffocating compositions and a thousand arts of chicanery, the knowledge of which he has acquired from experience. Sappers would be unable of themselves, without the aid of skilful miners, to execute that part of the covered road forming the descent into the ditch, and in various other portions of the road, the assistance of the miner is indispensable to the sapper; indeed without their joint labours and steady cooperation no besieger's approaches ever reached the walls of a fortress. A siege, scientifically prosecuted, though it calls for the greatest personal bravery, the greatest exertion and extraordinary labour in all employed, is beautifully certain in its progress and result.'

Unhappily this was never true of the British sieges in the Peninsula. Wellington had neither the trained sappers to accomplish the final stages of the siege, nor sufficient guns to silence those of the enemy: he always lacked time. In consequence he was forced to storm imperfectly blasted breaches from too far away. Even if he was successful, the cost of life, as at Badajoz, could be appalling, while he frequently risked a bloody repulse, as at Burgos and San Sebastian.

The number of trained engineers at his sieges is revealing. At the unsuccessful attempt on Badajoz in 1811 he had seventeen engineer officers distributed at two per brigade, excluding the commander in charge of the siege. He had besides twenty-five men of the Royal Corps of Military Artificers who were no more than storekeepers responsible for the engineer park and the issue of engineers' stores. He formed an *ad hoc* engineer unit by calling in forty-eight carpenters and forty-eight miners from his infantry battalions. At the sieges of Ciudad Rodrigo and Badajoz in 1812 his engineer resources were much the same and he supplemented them with twelve officers and 180 men culled again from the infantry, but these were no substitute for properly trained men.

After the atrocious number of casualties he suffered at the storm of Badajoz, he wrote home bitterly complaining of the lack of trained sappers, and War Office responded by creating the Royal Corps of Sappers and Miners. At the siege of San Sebastian he had 105 rank and file from the newly-formed corps, but their numbers were quite inadequate and the fortress fell only after the second attempt at a storm.

Guns were the other half of the siege equation. Siege-guns were heavy and difficult to move, requiring long trains of oxen if they travelled by road. The siege train sent out from England for the siege of Cuidad Rodrigo is fairly typical. Jones quotes this as being:

24-pounders iron	32
18-pounders iron	4
10 inch mortars iron	8
$5\frac{1}{2}$ inch mortars iron	20
$5\frac{1}{2}$ inch mortars brass	10
8 inch howitzers brass	2

However, for various reasons only thirty-eight of these were actually used at the siege and to man them there were 171 British gunners and 371 Portuguese, giving a total of 542 non-commissioned-officers and men; of these, Jones noted, '85 men over two reliefs for laboratory and magazine duties and escorts and to replace casualties'. The actual gun detachments were only six men strong; this may seem strangely small, but the guns were aimed with a deliberation that was almost pedantic, and care had to be taken to avoid overheating the barrels; as a result rates of fire as compared with field guns were slow. At San Sebastian a breaching battery of ten guns fired 350 rounds per gun over a period of $15\frac{1}{2}$ hours, giving an overall average of a little more than one round per gun every three minutes. Jones said of this, 'such a rate of firing was probably never equalled at any siege'.

2
BRITISH UNITS

Unfortunately only a few regiments can be featured here. We have therefore chosen English, Scottish, and Irish infantry regiments, a Scottish cavalry regiment, and the Royal Artillery. As is well known, there were many other famous regiments which fought with outstanding skill and bravery in these campaigns. Units such as the Rifle Brigade, Royal Scots, Middlesex, Royal Welsh Fusiliers, Northamptons, Worcesters, and Gloucesters, to name but a very few, earned fresh distinctions in critical battles.

The Black Watch

War with France provided a relief for the Black Watch from the distasteful duties of quelling disturbances caused by 'clearances' in the Highlands. Late in 1794 the 42nd joined an expedition to the Low Countries. Hardly had the regiment joined the army there than it was ordered to return to England to join a force destined to act against the French in the West Indies. This operation did not materialize, however, and after spending some time in the Channel Islands the Highlanders returned to Ostend to form part of the force under Lord Moira. This force at once joined the main army led by the Duke of York, command of the brigade comprising the 42nd and the Guards being given to Lieutenant-General Ralph Abercromby. After considerable skirmishing with the enemy the 42nd was present at the Battle of Geldermalsen in January 1795. The regiment itself did not suffer greatly, but French pressure was very severe and their forces were rapidly increasing in strength. The coming of winter added to the privations the British troops were suffering, and finally a general retreat was ordered. The troops reached Bremen at the beginning of April, and on the

14th of the month sailed for England. The losses suffered by the 42nd during this campaign were slight, only twenty-five being killed or perishing from disease.

On its return the regiment was brought up to strength from drafts supplied by other Highland units, raised the previous year and now disbanded; and it was detailed to join a very large expedition against the French in the West Indies. This undertaking was frustrated by a spell of the most appalling weather. Several starts were made, but many ships were sunk or went astray in storms. Finally, five companies of the Highlanders under Lieutenant-Colonel Dickson arrived at Gibraltar, while the other five reached Barbados on 9 February 1796. It was decided to make an assault on the island of St Lucia and, after some very sharp fighting, the regiment was sent from St Lucia to St Vincent. The 42nd was part of the invasion force which landed on 8 June and attacked the enemy two days later. There followed a period of very bitter fighting in the rough and broken interior of the island, with heavy casualties and, as always in the West Indies, mortality from disease extremely high.

The next island to be attacked was Trinidad, which surrendered without trouble; and from there another body of troops, again including the Royal Highlanders, was dispatched to Puerto Rico. But the defences of this place proved too strong for the modest army which had been sent, and it had to re-embark. The Highlanders returned to Martinique and thence back to England, but they left home shores almost at once to join the other five companies still serving on Gibraltar.

The regiment, some 1,000 strong, took part in the

(Above)

The Black Watch, though attacked before their square had time to
form, holding off French cavalry at Quatre Bras. Painting by
W. B. Wollen, R.I., 'The Black Watch at Bay'.

(Below)

The officer's gorget, derived from a piece of armour, worn in this
period fastened to the buttons at the top of the coat to denote rank.
Black Watch officer's sporran. The plate commemorates with a
Sphinx victory over the French in Egypt.

The shoulder-belt plate of an officer showing motto, badge, and regimental number, from the Peninsular War (1808–14).

expedition to Minorca which sailed from the Rock on 24 October 1797, reached the island on 6 November and landed almost unopposed. Citadella, the principal fortress, was invested on 14 November and surrendered the following day.

The resulting possession of Minorca was considered to be of the greatest strategic importance, for it was planned to use it as an assembly base for an army to act in the Mediterranean theatre of operations. The first enterprise was the relief of Genoa, but it started too late and Genoa surrendered to the French before the relief arrived.

On 2 October 1800 another operation was mounted, this time against the Spanish port of Cadiz. This, too, was abortive, the attackers being hurriedly withdrawn when it was discovered that plague was raging in the city. Back went the fleet to Gibraltar, and there it was given a new destination – Egypt. Shortly before Christmas, anchor was raised and, after pausing at a Turkish port in Greece, the fleet

Officer's uniform at the beginning of the Revolutionary Wars (1792). The officer is wearing the new-style 'little kilt', which replaced the belted plaid. The half-plaid worn from the shoulder to the waist is a reminder of the old garment. The bonnet too has changed, becoming higher and more shaped. (Youens/Osprey)

arrived off the Egyptian coast on 1 March 1801. Carrying the 42nd as part of the reserve, the great array of ships anchored in Aboukir Bay.

Naturally, this landing, opposed by a prepared and determined French army, proved costly; it was, however, completely successful. Casualties were

Corporal charging with bayonet fixed. His uniform is that worn before the Peninsular War (1808). Bad supply in the Spanish Peninsula led to drastic changes in uniform. (Youens/Osprey)

This private of 1815 is wearing equipment consisting of blanket on top of knapsack, haversack on left side, and water canteens. His rifle is the general issue Brown Bess. (Youens/Osprey)

The chevrons on the right arm show that this man is a sergeant, as does his half-pike or spontoon. He wears the 'hummel' bonnet of ostrich feathers, with a detachable peak tied at the back. His claymore can just be seen behind his kilt. (Youens/Osprey)

heavy, the 42nd losing nearly 200 of all ranks killed and wounded. The French soon decided to retreat to Alexandria where they had strong defences prepared. In this battle the Highlanders fought skilfully and unflinchingly to repel the French assault. After Alexandria, in which the regiment had fifty-four killed and 261 wounded, Cairo fell in due course: the situation left the French no alternative to capitulation. For their part in the campaign the Highlanders received the Sphinx and Egypt as their colours. Among the first to return to Britain, in December 1802, they stayed there until September 1805 when they were sent, with a resurrected second battalion whose final muster produced 1,300 men, to reinforce the garrison at Gibraltar.

In 1808 after Sir Arthur Wellesley's victory at Vimeiro, the 1st Battalion of the Highlanders came up from Gibraltar to join the British Army under the command of Sir John Moore in Portugal. The initial aim was for the British forces to unite with the Spanish armies in the field, but on his move towards Salamanca, the first point of concentration, Moore and his men found nothing of the Spanish troops who were supposed to join them. On the contrary, from every side came news of the destruction or dispersal of British forces.

Moore determined to maintain his advance. On 21 December he was met by the supporting force of Sir David Baird, thus bringing his army to a grand total of over 28,000 men. But on the 23rd Moore arrived at Sahagun, to learn that Napoleon himself with 40,000 men was in full march from Madrid. The inevitable retreat began on 24 December, and bitter medicine it was to the troops. When the order was communicated to the 42nd, the ground was littered with muskets the Highlanders had flung down in disgust. In many regiments discipline completely disappeared; and in dreadful winter conditions of snow and blizzard the army retreated 250 miles through the mountainous country of Galicia. With morale deteriorating daily, and with completely inadequate provisions, it was rather surprising that any troops remained in formation. Finally, after privations rivalling those experienced by the French in their retreat from Moscow a few years later, the British reached Corunna and turned to meet the pursuing French.

The British, after hours of severe and sustained fighting around the town, beat the French back at nightfall so that the evacuation was not opposed.

Having suffered 200 casualties in the battle, the 42nd arrived in England. The following summer saw the regiment back in Holland in the ill-famed Walcheren expedition. In six weeks it had suffered so heavily from the merciless Walcheren fever that on its return to this country only 200 men were left fit, even though it had hardly been in action. Much needed recruiting then took place in Edinburgh.

In the meantime the 2nd battalion, which had been stationed in Ireland since 1805, had been sent to join Wellington in Portugal. It took part there in many famous battles, including Busaco in 1810; garrisoned the defensive lines of Torres Vedras; and withstood the French cavalry at Fuentes d'Onoro. In May 1812 the 1st Battalion came to the Peninsula, where it amalgamated with the 2nd. The cadre of the 2nd returned to Britain, leaving the strengthened 1st with more than 1,100 men. The renewed battalion took part in the victory at Salamanca, as well as the less successful sequel when, after occupying Madrid, the army was forced to abandon the siege of Burgos in order to winter in Portugal. The Black Watch who had been at the front of the assault on the castle, had lost 300 men in one attack.

The next year, when Wellington made his victorious way through Spain to France, the 42nd were with him at Vitoria, the Nivelle, where they lost thirty men, Orthez, and finally at Toulouse. There the regiment, leading the attack, met bitter opposition: hardly 100 of their 500 men succeeded in reaching a French redoubt – only to find that the enemy had fled. The day's fighting took the heavy toll of fifty-four Highlanders killed and 267 wounded.

On the following day Toulouse was entered and within a week the French armies in the south had surrendered. The Highlanders were sent home, this time to Ireland, where they were reinforced by the men of the 2nd Battalion, previously sent home from the Peninsula, and now disbanded at Aberdeen. The regiment was again a single battalion.

On 1 March 1815 Napoleon landed in France from Elba; by 20 May he was in Paris. The pipes of war were again sounding for the 42nd, and yet again the regiment found itself in the Low Countries, initially stationed at Brussels.

On 13 June Wellington wrote from Brussels that it was unlikely there would be any immediate action from Bonaparte. But two days later the French, in great strength, crossed the frontier and flung themselves upon the Allies, who were widely dispersed and far from their concentration points. Wellington's reconnaissance was faulty and he was late in receiving definite knowledge of the French onslaught.

Brigaded with the 1st, 44th, and 92nd Regiments under Sir Denis Pack, the 42nd marched from Brussels at 4.00 a.m. on 16 June. By early afternoon, Picton's division, to which the brigade belonged, arrived at Quatre Bras in time to provide valuable assistance to the Prince of Orange, whose men were under attack by Marshal Ney. After sunset the fighting ended, with Ney finally realizing the impossibility of success and withdrawing his forces to a defensive line.

The murderous nature of the fighting at Quatre Bras had been almost without precedent. Not far short of 300 officers and men had been killed or wounded and never was a regiment more deserving of being singled out for praise than was the 42nd in Wellington's report.

The Battle of Waterloo took place two days later, on the morning of 18 June after a night of torrential rain and thunderstorms. Wellington's army lay along the ridge of Mont St Jean, awaiting the attack of the French forces assembled across the valley to their front.

The battle opened at Hougoumont in the middle of the morning; it was not until the early afternoon that Bonaparte attacked the farm of La Haye Sainte in the British centre. The battle for possession was eventually won by the French, but only at the price of being too exhausted and ill-supported to exploit the success substantially. At the climax of the battle the final attack, that by the Imperial Guard, was repulsed, and at once the French were everywhere in retreat. The battle was won.

The 42nd was not as heavily engaged as at Quatre Bras, but its fifty killed and wounded was a high enough total considering the casualties of the fighting two days before.

Following Waterloo, the 42nd joined in the general Allied advance to Paris, and after some months there returned home at the end of 1815 for a period of about ten years' peace-time soldiering.

Uniforms

In the 1790s the officers' dress had changed markedly. The little kilt had by now replaced the traditional belted plaid which had doubled as a blanket. This was pleated at the rear and the pleats stitched together, like the present-day Highland kilt. The separate piece of material attached to the belt below the coat, and to the left shoulder at the rear, is a half-plaid. Whereas also the bonnet had been flat, it became now rather higher, shaped, and had a diced band. Its tuft of feathers had grown larger. The coat collar was now a stand-up one, and the blue facings ornamented with square-ended loops. The sporran was probably of spotted seal fur.

During the years in Spain the uniform was subjected to drastic alterations, particularly hitting the other ranks. The impossibility of obtaining fresh clothing supplies made it inevitable that the traditional uniform should become sadly mutilated. It is said that, alone of the Highland regiments, the Black Watch managed to preserve the wearing of the kilt in reasonably good order.

The detachable peak to the bonnet and grey gaiters were adopted during the Peninsular War. The uniform coat was ornamented with bastion loops (pointed ends) on the buttonholes. A grey blanket rolled on top of the knapsack and haversack of rough fustian material worn with a water-canteen on left side made up the soldier's equipment on active service.

The sergeant of a battalion company wore the 'hummel' bonnet with ostrich feathers and a detachable peak tied on with tapes hanging down at the back. No sporrans were worn on active service. By this time there was a thin black edging to the pattern of the hose. Sergeants carried the half-pike as well as the claymore, and like the officers wore a crimson sash with a blue stripe, the 'facing colour', over the left shoulder.

The Coldstream Guards

Once Pitt had taken the decision to oppose the French in 1793 with Britain firmly committed to the anti-French Alliance, the Guards regiments were put on a war footing and the first battalions of all three regiments mobilized. At the same time their grenadier companies were united into a single grenadier battalion to form a species of élite body of shock troops (a common arrangement throughout the eighteenth century). Later, a fourth company consisting of the light troops of all three second battalions was added to the grenadiers, the whole forming a complete battalion.

The Coldstream drummer's uniform in 1790 is similar in many respects to that worn in modern times. The bearskin is brushed upwards over a red crown; the coat is liberally adorned with white lace worked with blue fleurs-de-lis. In full dress, white spatterdashes are worn. (Roffe/Osprey)

This Coldstream Guard grenadier of the beginning of the Peninsular War (1808) is from a flank company, as his blue-winged epaulettes laced with white show. He wears the bearskin, not yet issued to the battalion companies. (Roffe/Osprey)

The Guards Brigade was quickly moved to the Continent, and was posted to face the northern frontier of France where, on 8 May, the Coldstreamers went into action against well-defended

French entrenchments – which had already repulsed three assaults by other Allied troops. The 600 Coldstreamers first drove the enemy back, but combined musketry and cannon fire from a cleverly

All drum-majors wore elaborately ornamented uniforms. Gold lace is used on the Coldstreamer's coat in quantity. Note that the Wellington (or Belgic) shako, introduced in 1812, is also ornamented. White spatterdashes almost to the thigh are worn in place of his black gaiters in full dress. (Roffe/Osprey)

The Coldstream Guard officer is wearing the double-breasted coatee introduced in 1812. He is wearing a gold gorget below the white frill of his shirt; his epaulettes of the grenadier company are similar to those of all flank companies. His boots are black Hessian and have gold tassels. (Roffe/Osprey)

concealed flanking battery caused heavy losses and forced them to retire with seventy casualties.

The Coldstreamers were next employed at the siege of Valenciennes but were soon detached to join the force detailed to besiege Dunkirk. On 18 August the Guards had to go to the assistance of some Dutch troops under severe enemy pressure at Lincelles. The Dutch, making a rapid retreat, left the British to face

upon the regiment for active service followed each other rapidly and in 1800 the 1st Battalion sailed with the expedition to be made against Vigo. When this proved impracticable, the fleet continued on into the Mediterranean, bound for Egypt, for the troops to form part of Sir Ralph Abercromby's army. There followed tedious months at sea until a landing was made at Aboukir Bay on 8 March 1801, the battle in which Abercromby lost his life, after gaining the victory. Fighting lasted until the end of the year, even though Alexandria surrendered on 1 September. At the conclusion of the campaign the Coldstream Guards returned to England, with a short stay at Malta *en route*.

Private of grenadier company, Coldstream Guards, wearing the bearskin. His flintlock has a bayonet fixed by two loose rings. To the right of his shoulder-belt plate is a match-case, used with the old matchlock musket, but by this time purely decorative. (National Army Museum)

The first of two State Colours of the Coldstream Guards, which they have in addition to their ordinary colours. It is made of two sheets of crimson taffeta embroidered in gold, with the sphinxes in silver. The Crown and Garter Star is in full colour.

the enemy; but, advancing with levelled bayonets, the Coldstreamers and the rest of the brigade dashed at the French and scattered them.

Two miserable years followed in the Low Countries before the British Army retreated to Bremen to recross the Channel. The Coldstream Guards reached England in May 1795. They returned to Holland in 1799, forming part of two Guards brigades which fought with distinction at the Helder, Bergen, and Alkmaar before being recalled to England. Calls

Two expeditions were made by the 1st Battalion during 1805 and 1807, the first to Bremen and the second to Denmark; but on both occasions they returned to England without having been actively engaged. In January 1809, however, the battalion – numbering some 1,100 officers and men – brigaded with the 1st Battalion Scots Guards, sailed for the Spanish Peninsula, for the long series of operations culminating four years later with Wellington's drive across the Pyrenees into France. In May the brigade

The flintlock replaced the matchlock as firing mechanism and was used throughout the eighteenth century and half the next.

was at Coimbra in Portugal, the starting-point for the British advance to Oporto. In the following action the light company of the Coldstream Guards was first across the River Douro, before the whole regiment united to chase the French through the streets and into the open country beyond. The enemy made good their retreat by burning their baggage and escaping on goat-tracks through the frontier mountains.

On 27 and 28 July the regiment formed part of the centre of the British Army facing a powerful French force at Talavera. During the two days of the battle, three concentrated attacks were made on the British line by almost the entire French infantry. At one point only Wellington's quick action in moving his small reserve prevented the complete dislocation of his line. Another time the Coldstreamers, having halted an enemy thrust, rushed forward with the bayonet into range of enemy cannon fire, and counter-attack by foot and horse. Despite heavy losses they restored the situation, and after regrouping they returned to the offensive with a rush, driving the enemy before them. The regiment's casualties were very high, however, with thirty-six officers and men killed, and 263 wounded. Wellington, never lavish with his praise, included in his General Order on the battle a description of the charge as 'a most gallant one'.

Two further companies of the Coldstream Guards, this time from the 2nd Battalion, came out to Spain in March 1810 and were sent to reinforce the British garrison at Cadiz.

On 26 September Marshal Masséna and the French Army were halted by Wellington on the rocky slopes of Busaco. For two days the British held off the French attacks, with the Coldstreamers active on their stretch of front, until their position was outflanked and they drew back to the fortified lines of Torres Vedras in Portugal. Over the next few months frequent sorties were made to keep the French on the alert, and in November 1810 the Coldstreamers participated in a very successful harrying attack. At last, with all provisions exhausted and his army reduced to desperate straits, Masséna began to retreat on 5 March 1811. Efforts were made to convert his withdrawal into a rout. The Coldstream Guards took a prominent part in the pursuit, which was so close and sustained that the French had to destroy all their baggage and much ammunition when making good their crossing of the River Coa.

Meantime, on 4 March 1811, the two companies of the 2nd Battalion from Cadiz had fought the Battle of Barrosa, overwhelming a strong force of French in one notable charge.

On 3 May Masséna turned at bay and delivered a series of tremendous, but unsuccessful, attacks on Wellington, whose army was about the village of Fuentes d'Onoro. After a day's respite the battle was renewed on the 5th. The Coldstreamers were posted at some distance from the main scene of action and consequently suffered only slightly, although at one stage having to drive off with musketry a French cavalry charge. At length Masséna, not daring to maintain the struggle and running short of ammunition, withdrew on 8 May with far heavier losses than Wellington.

Coming out of winter quarters for the 1812 campaign, the regiment was employed in siege operations – first at Ciudad Rodrigo during January, then for the murderous business of the siege of Badajos, which fell on 6 April.

The summer was occupied with the operations against Marshal Marmont, a clever and accomplished soldier now in command of the French Army. The opposing armies, after some preliminary marching and manoeuvring, came to grips at Salamanca on 22 July.

Much of the heaviest fighting took place about the village of Arapiles where the light company of the Coldstream Guards was subjected to repeated attacks. They held out stoutly, and the regiment was the subject of a highly laudatory reference by Wellington in his report on the battle. Altogether it was a tremendous defeat for the French who lost 15,000 men in killed, wounded, and prisoners, as well as many guns and two of the cherished regimental 'eagles'.

The year's campaigning ended with the unsuccessful siege of Burgos, after which the army returned to winter quarters.

In the spring of 1813 the British were quickly on the move again, and on 21 June the victory of Vitoria was the immediate preliminary to a crossing of the Pyrenees. To secure his rear, Wellington laid siege in August to the great fortress of San Sebastian, a castle surrounded by the town of San Sebastian, itself protected by stout walls. As soon as a breach had been opened in the town walls by artillery bombardment, a detachment of two officers, two sergeants, a drummer, and fifty men of the Coldstream Guards volunteered to take part in storming it. The 'forlorn hope', as it was appropriately named, was the first unit into the breach. Finally, on 31 August, the defence cracked, and the town was taken. The castle surrendered some days later, but more than half the Coldstreamer detachment had fallen dead or wounded.

The battalion rejoined the field army now pressing forward through the mountain barrier, and before long France lay before the invading army. First came the crossing of the Nive, then the Nivelle, and the British columns were marching hard for Bayonne. By 23 March the troops were approaching the city, but first the River Adour had to be crossed on pontoons. Among the leading troops to cross, the light company of the Coldstreamers, together with men of the Scots Guards, were attacked by French infantry, who, after a volley, came rushing in with fixed bayonets. After a hard fight the French retreated, leaving the British to consolidate the crossing during that night and the following day. By 27 March the blockade of Bayonne was complete. This was the Coldstream Guards' last action of the war. The Battle for Orthez on 27 February had already been won by Wellington, and on 10 April he attacked the French at Toulouse. It was a costly encounter, more so to the British than to the French, but it was nevertheless a victory – the last of the Peninsular War. In July 1814 the Coldstream Guards returned to England after nearly six years of the hardest campaigning the regiment had ever experienced.

Meanwhile, on 13 December 1813, six companies of the 2nd Battalion had been sent to Holland. On 8 and 9 March 1814 they were in action against the strong fortress of Bergen-op-Zoom, an ill-judged venture; the British forces suffered extremely heavy losses, and the attempt was a failure. On 4 August, however, the six companies were moved to Brussels and shortly afterwards the battalion was completed by the arrival of the headquarters component and the four other companies from England. It was thus happily at full strength when the news sped across Europe that Napoleon had escaped from banishment on the island of Elba and had arrived in Paris. Again battle had to be joined and at once the battalion was moved to a more advanced position at Enghien. There it remained until 16 June 1815 when Napoleon's onslaught fell upon the scattered British and Prussian Armies.

At Quatre Bras Wellington grimly held off a furious attack by Marshal Ney while his supporting brigades and divisions made forced marches to join him. Roused before daybreak the Coldstream Guards – forming the 2nd Guards Brigade with the Scots Guards – marched twenty-five miles through the heat in full marching order to arrive at Quatre Bras at 4.00 p.m. For hours the men with Wellington had held on under continual attack from cavalry and infantry, and the issue was in the balance. But when the Guards arrived the scene changed, defence became offence, and in support of the 1st Guards

This trooper of the Greys, the only Scottish regular cavalry regiment, wears the fur cap permitted again in 1807, instead of the regulation cocked hat for dragoon regiments. In 1811 the white lace was replaced by two broad bands of yellow. (Youens/Osprey)

Brigade the Coldstreamers surged forward. It was the turning-point of the battle, and everywhere the battered enemy fought to the point of exhaustion.

But the success at Quatre Bras was counter-balanced by Napoleon's defeating the Prussians at Ligny on the same day. When news of this was brought to Wellington on the 17th, he gave orders for retreat to the Waterloo position. There, on the morning of 18 June, the British general drew up his somewhat heterogeneous army to meet the last grand attack of the French.

On the right front of the Allied position the farm – or chateau as it can also be called – of Hougoumont had been occupied by the light companies of the four Guards battalions, that from the Coldstream Guards being stationed in the buildings and gardens of the farm under Lieutenant-Colonel Macdonell. Loop-holes had been made in the walls, and the gates barricaded. The remainder of the Coldstream battalion was on a ridge just behind Hougoumont. Shortly after 11.00 a.m. the first attack on the farm was made by troops of Napoleon's brother Jerome. It was intended by the Emperor to be a diversionary move, but was converted into an all-out effort by the young man burning to make a name for himself, and continuous assaults broke upon the farm for many hours. Skirmishers crept through the under-growth of the near-by woods to fire at short range. Some Nassau infantry taking part in the defence were driven off, but Macdonell and his Coldstreamers counter-attacked immediately. They gained at least partial relief, but soon masses of French infantry occupied all the outbuildings of the farm and actually burst open the great gate and broke into the main courtyard. Again Macdonell and his men were on the scene and managed to close the gate.

At this point, reinforcements, including a company of Coldstreamers, came to the hard-pressed defenders and, together with the original garrison, they charged and drove back the French. The officer commanding the Coldstream Guards, Colonel Woodford, brought four more companies of his regiment into the fight. He made a desperate attempt to drive the French out of the wood about the farm, but the odds were too great and the Coldstreamers had to fall back into the buildings. Hour after hour the battle continued, with volleys at close range and hand-to-hand fighting with bayonet and musket-butt. The defence hung on courageously throughout the long day; evening came

at last and with it the defeat of the French Imperial Guard. The French began to fall back, slowly at first but then in complete disintegration. Hougoumont had been held but at a fearful cost – the Coldstream Guards had lost eight officers and 300 other ranks killed or wounded.

The battle over, the regiment took part in the advance on Paris which was entered in July. It remained there until February 1816 when it was posted to Cambrai. The regiment returned to London in November 1818.

Uniforms

A grenadier at the height of the Napoleonic Wars had the front of the short jacket ornamented with buttons and lace arranged in pairs. The blue-winged epau-lettes of the flank companies were laced with white, and the bearskin was ornamented with white cap lines, a white plume, and bore a small brass plate in the front. The bearskin itself was not issued to the whole regiment until considerably later, the battalion companies wearing the standard shako of the period.

In 1812 the Wellington or Belgic shako was introduced as a headdress, and this, too, was very elaborately ornamented. Made from black felt, it had a high false front and bore a brass plate in the shape of a shield surmounted by a crown with the Garter Star in the centre.

A brass plate was placed at the junction of the white crossbelts. Although a flintlock musket was carried at this period, the match-case was still worn on the crossbelt purely as an ornament.

The elaborate badge, peculiar to the Guards and denoting the wearer's rank or function, was worn on both upper arms. It consisted of three gold lace chevrons bearing the King's Colour with crossed swords beneath and surmounted by a crown. As an indication of the company to which he belonged, the colour sergeant wore a small silver grenade on each epaulette. The red coat was single-breasted, fastened in front with five pairs of regimental brass buttons decorated with gold lace, and had the skirts turned back to reveal white lining. There were two buttons at the back waist seams, and also two pocket-flaps edged with gold lace in four panels, each panel having a brass button in the centre. A crimson sash was worn around the waist, knotted on the left hip with two tassels hanging down at the side. In half and full dress, the 12-inch-high bearskin cap bearing the Royal

Charge of the Greys at Waterloo, assisted by the 92nd Highlanders (later the Gordons). The ferocity of this attack resulted in the taking of many French infantrymen and the capture of two 'Eagles'. From a print after Stanley Berkeley. (National Army Museum)

(Below)
This painting of a 'Charge of the Scots Greys at Waterloo' by Lady Butler conveys well the psychological effect of a cavalry charge; however, a charge out of control would leave a vulnerable gap in the battle-line. (National Army Museum)

The officer of the Greys is wearing the uniform used at the end of the eighteenth century. His crimson sash is worn over the coat. The bicorn hat is still worn although impractical; when riding it was turned sideways for convenience. (Youens/Osprey)

Private of the Greys wearing the bearskin headdress. The badge on the front is the thistle within the circle of St Andrew. Both the shoulder-belt and the waistbelt are of white leather. (Youens/Osprey)

The back view of an officer of the Greys. The bicorn hat, no longer worn on field service, is adorned with high white feather plumage for ceremonial wear. The black sabretache can be clearly seen. (Youens/Osprey)

Arms and regimental title on a brass plate was worn, while on service this was replaced by the Wellington shako with a white plume. Full dress also included the thigh-length white spatterdashes in place of half-dress gaiters, while on active service yet another difference appearing by this time would have been charcoal-grey trousers over black gaiters. Weapons included – for Foot Guards and senior NCOs – the sword of the 1803 pattern, with brass hilt and fishskin grip bound by twisted silver wire, and having a slightly curved blade encased in a black leather scabbard with two brass mounts. The topmost of these mounts bore a stud which fitted into the 'frog' on the crossbelt. The most distinctive weapon was the infantry sergeant's pike – regulation issue from 1792 to 1830 – known from 1803 as the spontoon.

The spontoon was a modification of the long halberd which had been carried by sergeants since 1700. For action, this weapon would be used to form up around the colours to ward off a cavalry attack. In 1792 sergeants ceased to carry the halberd, which was replaced by this half-pike (or spontoon), permitted now only to NCOs of Grenadier and centre companies. Light company NCOs carried rifle muskets.

The officer of the Grenadier company in 1815, in service or half dress, wore a double-breasted scarlet coatee of the 1812 pattern, with two rows of ten gilt buttons arranged in pairs. His coat was buttoned over so that the facings and lace were almost concealed, with the exception of the blue lapel facings, but the collar was left open to show a white shirt frill, below which was worn a small gold gorget. This latter was indicative of the officer's status and derived from the last article of medieval armour to be utilized. Its presence usually indicated that the bearer was on duty. At the back of the coatee there were two buttons at the waist seams, and two pocket-flaps edged with gold lace, bearing four buttons spaced in pairs. A characteristic of all flank companies was the winged epaulettes. Those worn by the grenadier company were liberally laced in gold and bore a small grenade worked in gold wire. Around the waist was a crimson net sash, knotted on the left hip, with four tassels. When opened out, these tassels would appear at each corner, and the sash was often used to carry wounded officers from the field of battle as well as for pure decoration. In full dress this officer would wear white breeches and long white spatterdashes, buttoned on the outer side of each leg, extending to the thigh, with

a blue garter and gilt buckle worn below the knees. In half dress either black gaiters or black hessian boots with gold tassels at the front would be worn.

The greatcoat with cape was introduced during the Napoleonic Wars and was worn over the officer's service-dress uniform. Previous to this period there was no similar garment.

Royal Scots Greys *(Royal North British Dragoons)*
The Royal North British Dragoons were given the title of 2nd Dragoons (Royal Scots Greys) in 1877, but fellow soldiers had called them 'the Greys' since 1693.

In 1793 the Greys were augmented to nine troops, each of fifty-four non-commissioned officers and men, and soon after this four troops were placed on stand-by duty. On 9 July the move was made, the four troops embarked at Blackwall for Flanders, to join the British and Hanoverian armies under the Duke of York, mustering for operations against the French who were pressing northwards from their old frontiers. On 23 July the fortress of Valenciennes capitulated to the Duke of Coburg and it seemed that the French would probably be pushed back from the Low Countries, and that an invasion of the French homeland might be a feasible operation. About a week earlier, the four troops had landed at Ostend and had marched directly to join the army, arriving just before the fall of Valenciennes. This success was, unfortunately, the turning point; instead of pressing on for Paris the Allies temporized, adopting the plan of capturing Dunkirk. But since the Duke of York was provided with no siege train, the chances of capturing this well-defended fortress were small. Abandoning the attempt under pressure, the Greys spent the rest of the year as part of a skirmishing screen. Their one encounter with the French was a success, but in November all four troops moved back to Ghent. The five remaining in England were increased in strength to eighty men each.

After a fairly severe winter the Greys, in preparation for the 1794 campaign, moved from Ghent to Beveren in February, and in March took the field, shortly after receiving from England a welcome remount of seventeen men and forty-two horses – not an enormous reinforcement, it is true, but it did help to fill the gaps left through disease. In April, before their investment of the fortress of Landrecies, the Regiment supported some infantry in an attack on the villages of Vaux and Premont, and when the fortress was actually under siege, it joined the covering army nearby. On 26 April sharp action took place against a strong French force which advanced under the cover of a thick fog, but the assailants were flung back, and a fine cavalry charge accelerated an already rapid retreat.

After Landrecies surrendered, the Greys were sent by forced marches to the vicinity of Tournai, and took up a position in front of the town. The remainder of the army followed, and on 10 May the whole force, with the Greys positioned in the left rear, was fiercely attacked by the French. British and Hanoverian musketry was most effective and held up the assault, while the Greys, forming a brigade with two other dragoons regiments (one of them the Inniskillings, with whom they were to be gallantly associated in further battles), were sent to attack the French right flank, the Duke of York guiding the advance personally. The French crumbled before the on-slaught, fleeing in utter confusion and abandoning thirteen pieces of artillery. The loss to the Greys was slight – only twenty officers and men killed or wounded.

Despite this success the French pressure increased steadily as fresh reinforcements – the product of the organizing genius of Carnot, the French Minister of War – moved up towards the theatre of operations, and on 18 May the Duke of York suffered a serious reverse at Turcoing, his somewhat antiquated ideas of manoeuvre proving ineffective when matched against the skirmishers and sharpshooters pushed forward by the French. The campaign thereafter became a series of retreats and rearguard actions, in which the Greys played a prominent part. Forced back all the way to Holland, where the populace were very pro-French, and exposed to a really hard winter, with drenching rain and bitter cold, the morale of the British Army fell to a lamentably low level, illness and exhaustion being commonplace in horse and man. The season increased in severity with heavy snow and freezing temperatures, and great hardships were endured by the troops, since provisions were scarce and at times actually non-existent. During this dreadful time the Greys were at Nijmegen, but conditions became so impossible that a further retreat proved necessary and finally, in a very battered state, the army arrived at Bremen. The British troops saw no further action. During the summer of 1795 the four

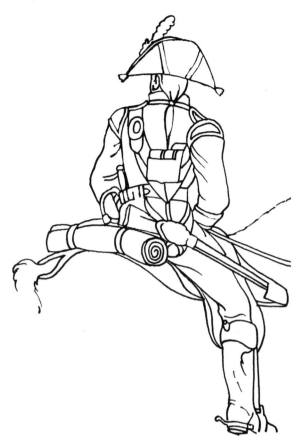

This sketch of a trooper of the Royal Scots Greys shows the equipment carried in the middle of the Napoleonic Wars. The hair, worn long in this illustration, became cut short 'in the modern style' in 1808.

troops of the Greys encamped in villages on the banks of the Weser until their embarkation in November for England. With the overseas troops now back in Britain the 9th was disbanded: the establishment was fixed at 679 officers and men.

For almost twenty years the Royal North British Dragoons stayed in the British Isles.

From time to time the composition of the Regiment changed, and in April 1800 a tenth troop was added to the establishment, primarily in order to absorb a draft of eighty-one men received from units of the disbanded Fencible cavalry. With the signing of the Peace of Amiens on 27 March 1802 and the conclusion of hostilities with the French Republic, the strength of the Regiment was reduced to eight troops numbering 553 officers and men. The period of peace, however, was to last only fourteen months, and in May 1803 there was a fresh declaration of war against France.

The many buttons on the side of the trousers of this trooper of the Greys enabled them to fit tightly. The bearskin can be seen with its cover off and, in the inset, when covered with an oilskin.

Accordingly, back went the establishment to the wartime strength of ten troops, and the Regiment was at the greatest strength it had ever enjoyed – over 1,000 officers and men. For two years it was stationed at Canterbury in Kent, forming part of the force designed to repel Napoleon's threatened invasion. When the French Emperor marched off into central Europe on his career of conquest, precautions were somewhat relaxed and the Greys were moved to quarters at Ipswich and Colchester.

The risk of invasion seemed to be relatively negligible. The establishment was once again reduced. A move to Ireland took place in 1808, and during the quartering of the Regiment in that country an important order was promulgated, to wit, that the men's hair, formerly plaited and powdered, was henceforth to be cut short, a modernization which saved the troops both time and money.

Throughout the course of the Peninsular War, during which many of the Greys' fellow regiments were winning fame and gaining battle honours, the Regiment had to endure the frustration of being kept at home, moving as usual from barracks to barracks, certainly chafing at the enforced inaction.

A further reduction to eight troops or less than six hundred men was authorized in July 1814, but it was speedily countermanded in the following spring when the Emperor Napoleon escaped from Elba and arrived in Paris. The Regiment was then brought up to war strength and simultaneously, to the great joy of the Greys, six of the troops were ordered to prepare for foreign service. Indeed, during the course of April 1815 they sailed from Gravesend, landed at Ostend, and took up quarters near Ghent. Brigaded with the Royal Dragoons and the Inniskilling Dragoons under Major-General Sir William Ponsonby, the Greys now formed part of that famous unit to be known – from the number of nationalities of the regiments comprising it – as the Union Brigade.

Fame at Quatre Bras and Waterloo was dearly bought by the Dragoons. Their sterling work at Waterloo was all but turned to disaster when their charge, which tore apart the French battalions, went too far, leaving Napoleon a gap into which he tried to force his light and heavy cavalry. French artillery continued to decimate the Greys. At the end of the battle when the Prussians had arrived, scarcely one effective squadron could be produced. The victory, though it gave the Regiment its captured French 'Eagle', cost ninety-seven wounded and 104 dead or dying.

Uniforms
From 1768 onwards the private wore the bearskin headdress which had been authorized in place of the old cloth grenadier cap. The coat was red, with turned-down collar with two white loops on each side; blue, white-embroidered cloth epaulettes were worn on each shoulder; cuffs were blue with two pairs

of loops. Waistcoat, breeches and turnbacks were all white. The bearskin cap bore the badge of the Thistle within the circle of St Andrew on the plate, and there was a white plaited cord at the rear, ending in a tassel which can be seen projecting from the side of the headdress. The hair was worn in a plait turned up at the back. The crossbelt was white leather as was the belt worn about the waist.

The regulation cocked hat of the period was quite plain, but had a red-and-white plume. The jacket was scarlet; the collar was blue with two gold lace bars. There were gold chain wings on the shoulders and four pairs of gold lace loops on the front of the coat. A white pouch-belt with oval gilt plate was worn over the left shoulder, and it bore a small black pouch hanging just on the right hip. The sash was crimson with the ends hanging to the wearer's right, and the coat turnbacks were blue, bordered with gold lace and ornamented at their junction. White gloves were worn, white breeches and knee-boots.

Again in 1807 we find a return to an individual headdress, once more a variety of the fur cap. Prior to this year the regulation cocked hat of the dragoon regiments had been worn for some time. The white lace ornamenting the front of the jacket appears, in one contemporary source, to have been worn in pairs of loops, and red, white-laced shoulder wings can be seen. In 1811 this white lace was replaced by broad stripes of yellow lace running vertically down the front of the coat and extending round the skirts. A brownish goatskin covered the saddle and a red cloak was rolled and strapped over the pistol-holsters carried in front of the saddle. The collar, cuffs, and shoulder-straps were blue, the collar being ornamented with a pair of white lace loops, and the shoulder-straps also edged white. In this year 'milled kersey breeches' were proposed for regimental wear instead of 'shag breeches', the price of the coarse wool from which the latter were made having increased astronomically. Where the rank and file wore white lace, the officers wore gold. Horse housings were of blue, edged with lace and bearing the badge of the Thistle on a red background within a blue circle. Holster-caps were blue, edged with similar lace with 'II.D' thereon, and a 'G.R.' monogram in yellow. From 1729 the regulation horse for dragoons was to be 'a strong, well-bodied horse, 15 hands high'.

The Scotch Brigade (88th) and De Burgh's Regiment (94th)

Among the first of the new regiments raised in haste at the declaration of war against France in 1793 were De Burgh's on 25 September and, on the next day, the Scotch Brigade. These two regiments, later numbered 88 and 94, became united under the Cardwell reforms as the two regular battalions of the Con-

The green facings on the coat of this private of the Scotch Brigade in 1794 are reminders of the brigade's service to the Dutch. The red and white plume shows that he is of a battalion company. (Youens/Osprey)

naught Rangers. The Scotch Brigade had no less than twenty-six officers of the recently disbanded Scots Brigade which had existed since it was raised in 1572 for the Dutch War of Independence.

In the flurry of invasion scares so many units had been raised that few were up to strength. The Duke of York, recently appointed Commander-in-Chief, showed his administrative ability by amalgamating under-strength units. By the time the Scotch Brigade got to Gibraltar in 1796 it was a single battalion. After a few months it went to the Cape of Good Hope as reinforcements against a Dutch threat to recapture the colony; there it was brigaded with the 86th. In India also war was brewing against Tippoo Sultan. So now, with the 84th under the command of General Baird, the brigade made for Madras at the end of 1798. The last company did not arrive until the following February by which time six companies had already gone to join the march of the Grand Army on Seringapatam. This company managed to win considerable renown, however, as it was detached to take part in a remarkable naval action, the capturing of the French frigate, *La Forte*, with the men serving as marines on board the British frigate, *Sybille*. Under cover of darkness the British ship slipped close to *La Forte*, and after a fierce battle took the frigate. While the French lost sixty-five killed and eighty-five wounded, casualties on the *Sybille* were only five killed and sixteen wounded.

The advance on Seringapatam took nearly two months, using 37,000 troops, of whom slightly more than 5,000 were Europeans. Three of the four British battalions were formed into an assault brigade under Baird (the 12th, the 74th, and six companies of the Scotch Brigade, which mustered 559 all ranks with Major Skelly in command). The battalion commander on its formation commanded a brigade of Madras native troops throughout the campaign. Tippoo's available forces were numbered at 59,000 which included a large body of rocket troops. At the end of the fierce siege and assault which finally gained the town, the number of enemy dead was in the region of 10,000. The capture of Seringapatam cost the Grand Army over 1,500 casualties, of whom 367 died in the assault: the Scotch Brigade itself lost thirteen men killed and eighty wounded.

During the Mahratta War the Scotch Brigade led the assault at Asseerghur and were in the forefront of the Battle of Argaum. After the storming of Gawil-

The picture, 'Listing for the Connaught Rangers' painted by Lady Butler, although of a later date, well portrays the spirit and jauntiness of the new recruit.

ghur, a fortress previously considered impregnable, Major James Campbell and the light company under Captain Frederick Campbell received the special thanks of Major-General Wellesley. In 1851 the issue of an Indian medal was authorized and four officers and forty men of the battalion were alive to receive it.

In 1802, while the battalion was in Madras, it was given a new title – 94th (Scotch Brigade). The allocation of this low number caused much bitterness in a regiment that claimed more than ninety years' seniority over the Coldstream Guards. In 1808 the battalion returned to Dunbar in Scotland. Its services in India had not been forgotten by the East India Company on whose representation the following was published in the *London Gazette*, dated 16 April 1807: 'His Majesty has been graciously pleased to approve of the 94th Regiment bearing the Elephant on their Colours and on their Appointments as an honourable and lasting testimony of their distinguished Services in India.' It was also about this time that the title 'Scotch Brigade' was dropped from the Army List. Early in 1810 the 94th joined Sir Arthur Wellesley's army in the Peninsula.

The 88th Connaught Rangers, as they were later known, were already there. They had been raised by The Hon. John Thomas de Burgh, mainly in

73

The bloody siege and attack at Seringapatam in India is the subject of this painting. The Grand Army lost 1,500 men, and that of Tippoo Sultan 10,000, in the assault alone. (National Army Museum)

Print of the breach of Ciudad Rodrigo, a key fortress contested in the Peninsular War. After continual sieges it fell to Wellington's assault in 1813. (National Army Museum)

Picture of the castle at Badajoz being stormed by British troops in April 1812 with losses of 3,000 in the assault and 1,000 in the twenty-one day siege. (National Army Museum)

Painting of the battle of Salamanca, in which Wellington comprehensively outfought and outmanoeuvred Marmont. The Connaught Rangers have here captured 'Jingling Johnnie' from the French.

As a concession to the heat, the Scotch Brigade fought in India (1799–1807) in a shorter jacket, shorter gaiters, and a generally lighter uniform. (Youens/Osprey)

This private of a battalion company of the Scotch Brigade is dressed in the uniform worn towards the end of the Peninsular War. His shako is of the 'stovepipe' pattern, and his hair is now cut short. (Youens/Osprey)

Connaught in 1793, and took up their military home in Chatham. In the next year they were given the number 88th and packed off to suffer the terrible deprivations of the winter campaign in Holland under the Duke of York; but by the following April typhus forced the 88th to be withdrawn to England again. Out of 773 men 543 were unfit for duty. Ill fortune struck again in 1795 when under their new

commander Lieutenant-Colonel William Beresford they set off for the West Indies only to have their fleet scattered by a storm, which allowed just three ships to reach Grenada.

In 1796 the battalion was reunited in England, now with 400 men. After two years in Jersey they spent 1799 and 1800 stationed in Bombay, Ceylon, then Egypt under General Baird, and there they marched from the Red Sea to the Nile to reach Alexandria. On returning to England from Egypt in 1802, they spent four years in an anti-invasion role on the south-east coast. In September 1806 they embarked for a secret mission, originally to Chile; they did not sail for two months but when they did, it was to make the disastrous attempt on Buenos Aires. Out of a force of eight battalions and three cavalry regiments, two of which were dismounted, that sailed up the Rio de la Plata to attack the 15,000 Spaniards, 1,000 were killed and 2,000 taken prisoner. The Spanish losses are not known, other than that 1,000 of them were taken prisoner and they were deprived of thirty guns. The Connaught Rangers themselves had twenty officers killed and 200 men killed and wounded.

Defeated and humiliated, the British force made its way back to England, whence within the year the Rangers were sent to Lisbon to take part in the Peninsular War, this time with the Spanish as allies. They were attached for a time to the Portuguese army, since Lieutenant-General Beresford had been given command of the Portuguese.

The 88th displayed courage and steadiness throughout this campaign, beginning with the Battle of Talavera, and especially by valiant work at Busaco, while the 94th were distinguishing themselves in the siege of Cadiz. In 1810 the battalion joined the second brigade of 3 Division which was holding the forward sector of the Lines at Torres Vedras. Together they fought for four years in 'Picton's Fighting Division' besieging Badajoz and Ciudad Rodrigo. In the assault on the latter the 3rd Division was chosen as spearhead: the fortress fell after a famous struggle. During the whole siege Wellington's army lost 1,052 killed and wounded. The 88th had one officer and twenty men killed during the assault, with five officers and forty-six men wounded; the 94th, two officers killed and five wounded, and from the ranks thirteen died and forty-eight received wounds.

Amid the mud of Badajoz, the British must have lost in the region of 5,000 men: the 94th who had been last to cross the dam for the assault were spared the worst of the ordeal. The brunt, however, was borne by the 88th with the heaviest casualties of any battalion in the Division – sixteen officers killed or wounded, and more than 225 men.

1812 proved the turning point in the Peninsular War, for in the Battle of Salamanca Wellington showed convincingly that he could take on the French troops in open battle and beat them in manoeuvre. By nightfall on 22 July the French were in full retreat with losses of up to 15,000, about one third of the force with which they had started the day. The British, Spanish, and Portuguese with their force deprived by the battle of 5,000 men, but having won a signal victory, could feel well satisfied with their work. The campaign was not over: in October Wellington had to withdraw from the siege of Burgos in order to retreat into his winter quarters. The following summer, however, saw the French retreating over the Pyrenees after the Battle of Vitoria. Napoleon's abdication after the capture of Paris brought an end to the Connaught Rangers' heroic part in the war; they were fighting in Canada when news came of Bonaparte's hundred days and his final defeat at Waterloo.

Uniforms

Up to the year 1782 the Scots Brigade wore the uniform of the Dutch Army (it had been originally raised in 1572 for the Dutch War of Independence), but retained the scarlet of Great Britain. So in the early eighteenth century the uniform was similar to any other line regiment, with the caps of the Grenadiers bearing the Dutch Arms. The facings of the scarlet coats (to distinguish the regiments of the Brigade) varied from time to time. When Dundas became commander of one regiment in 1777 it became the 'blue regiment' from its blue facings, which had previously been green and, before that, yellow. The details of the musketeer's uniform were given as: Hat: Black with white lace, black cockade and white tassels with a red heart. Coat: Red with lace and pewter buttons; white shoulder-straps; light blue hearts on the white turnbacks. Waistcoat and Breeches: Greyish white. Gaiters: White with pewter buttons. Shoes: Black. Sword: Brass-hilted, sword knot of white leather with a different coloured tassel for each company. Belt: White, the waistbelt having a brass beltplate.

The uniform of a grenadier in the same regiment was somewhat more elaborate – Bearskin: Black with red bag and white tassel. Coat: Red with light blue lapels and cuffs. On the lapels, seven loops of plain white lace $(1+2+2+2)$. On the cuffs, two loops and three pewter buttons on the sleeves. Under the lapels two loops of a special pattern, broad with white tassels on both sides and a light blue loop worn in the lace. On the left shoulder a plain white strap; on the right shoulder a white epaulette with a light blue worn in the lace, and white lace loops. Waistcoat and gaiters as for the musketeer's uniform. Sword: Brass-hilted, with white sword-knot and orange tassels. Belt: White with brass buckle on the waistbelt, and brass match-case on the shoulder belt.

In April 1809, shortly after the 94th returned from India, the War Office issued an order that the regiment along with five others would discontinue wearing the kilt to 'facilitate' transfers from the English militia. This order must have caused much amusement in the orderly-room of the 94th. The other five regiments were Highland Regiments, but the 94th had been raised as a Lowland Regiment and wore the normal British Line Regiment's uniform. When the Scotch Brigade was raised in 1793, twenty-four former Scots Brigade officers found themselves posted to the three battalions. Other regiments raised at the same time wore yellow facings and it is perhaps more than a coincidence that the Scotch Brigade sported the distinctive green facing (described as Lincoln green) that had been worn by many of the officers while in the Dutch service. The details of the officer's coat for the 88th Regiment in 1807 were 'Scarlet coat lined with white. White turnbacks sewed down. Yellow lapels 10 holes. Yellow collar, 1 hole and small button each end. Yellow cuffs, 4 holes – by 2 all over.' The details included a white, short, single-breasted cashmere waistcoat and breeches, blue pantaloons, trimmed with broad and narrow braid; plus thirty-eight large, and three small regimental buttons and silver epaulettes and ornaments. The men's lace at this date was two black, two red, and one yellow stripes, while the 94th was one red stripe. A few years later (in 1813) the lace on an officer's coat of the 94th is noted as $9\frac{1}{2}$–12 yards fine check lace. Skirt and other details include: single ornaments, two single-leaved thistles on green, while the epaulette was gold fine check wire strap, round top, corded with a pointed, flat feather crescent and a rose in centre and looped all round.

When the Scotch Brigade was raised in 1793 their uniform was that of a British Line Regiment, but the distinctive green facings form a link with their ancient origins. The white lace on the coat is formed in square loops and set in pairs; the coat buttons are of pewter. The crossbelt plate is of engraved brass, but without the numerals '94'. The red and white plume on the hat indicates that the soldier belongs to one of the 'battalion' companies and not to one of the flank companies.

A soldier of the 94th during the latter part of the Peninsular War would be wearing the 'universal' pattern shako with the crown and Royal Cipher on the shako plate. The brass crossbelt plate would bear the elephant and '94' in the centre within a wreath, with 'Scotch Brigade' below. The hair was still powdered, but worn short without a queue.

The uniform worn in India was lighter in weight and the scarlet coats were much shorter. The officer wore gold lace, and the buttons on the coat were gilt; the hatband was also of gold lace. An obvious concession to the hot climate was short gaiters and white cotton drill trousers and waistcoat.

The Buffs

On 31 August 1782 an order was issued affiliating the Buffs to East Kent, with the necessary insertion in the title. Kent is thought to have been chosen by the Colonel of the Regiment, Major-General Style, who in fact lived in West Kent and may perhaps never have seen his regiment, for they were overseas throughout his colonelcy. All the same, recruits were gathered from whichever part of the country offered the best yield.

Returned to England in 1790, the Buffs now sported black cockades and feathers (the latter at the men's expense) in their black cocked hats, and their coats were cut back like morning coats and surmounted by white crossbelts, with a plate at the intersection. Thus attired, they set off in September 1793 to fight the French revolutionaries, only to endure some futile voyaging back and forth across the Channel, which ended with their return to England badly smitten by the dread 'jail fever', typhus. In July 1794 they joined the army of Frederick Augustus, the 'noble Duke of York', in Flanders and in April 1795 they limped into Bremen for evacuation to Yarmouth. They had suffered terrible losses from frostbite and starvation and hardly had a fight with the enemy.

In October 1795 they embarked for the West Indies, as part of an enormous expedition. A storm

'The Buffs in Flanders' painted by R. Simkin. Two officers in different headgear are conversing in the foreground. This was not the memory most British had of marshy Holland.

The Buffs racing to prevent the French forcing an entry into the seminary at the River Douro outside Oporto in 1809. Picture by Christopher Clark.

This picture by W. B. Wollen shows resolute defence of the colours at Albuhera. By incredible heroism the colours remained intact but only eighty-five out of 728 Buffs survived the battle.

wrought havoc. One shipload of Buffs (headquarters and five companies) rode it unscathed and reached Barbados in late January 1796, whence they were despatched to subdue a rising in St Vincent. The ship carrying the other five companies was forced back to England and did not reach the West Indies until March. They were directed to Grenada and had a very sticky day's fighting in driving out the Negro rebels who had seized the island. The Buffs then occupied several other islands, perhaps deriving some relief from the cotton trousers and white hats they were authorized to wear. They returned to England in June 1802, leaving behind many comrades stricken by yellow fever.

They returned at a time of radical alteration in dress and probably received new uniform soon after their arrival. The cocked hats of the soldiers, though retained by officers, gave way to the peaked stovepipe cap, which had a plate in front for the dragoon and was also adorned by a plume, white for the Grenadier Company, green for the Light (formed in 1770), and red and white for the other companies. The cut-away coat was replaced by a single-breasted coatee, cut to the waist in front and to the seat behind, with high buff collar, buff cuffs, and bars of buff across the front. Officers wore double-breasted coats of longer skirting and without the bars across the front. They had silver epaulettes. The soldiers still wore breeches and gaiters, but were to exchange them for dark grey trousers some time after reaching the Peninsula. The officers took to blue pantaloons and Hessian boots.

After a brief peace the war was resumed in May 1803, and the Buffs again raised a second battalion, which first stood ready to defend Kent and was subsequently relegated to draft-finding duties. The

1st Battalion journeyed to Germany in November 1805, to defend Hanover on the line of the Weser, but were obliged to return after three months, without being closely engaged. They moved to Ireland and from here, in December 1807, to Madeira, by invitation of the island's owner, Portugal. They were needed next year in Portugal itself, and as they arrived at Lisbon on 1 September 1808 the French sailed away in British ships with all their arms and

The officer of the Buffs in 1792 wears a silver gorget beneath his white lace frill and a white metal shoulder-belt plate. The facings are of course buff-coloured, as is the waistcoat.
(Youens/Osprey)

The Buffs' sergeant, recognized by his three chevrons and spontoon, wears the shorter coatee adopted in 1803, and the stovepipe shako with which he was issued in 1800.
(Youens/Osprey)

The Buffs' officer of 1803 is wearing the long uniform coat which had been replaced altogether for other ranks by the short coatee: on duty the officer would also wear the shorter coat. (Youens/Osprey)

The uniform of the Buffs' private at the beginning of the war against France is similar to that of the officer; the soldier has crossed shoulder-straps in place of the officer's single sword-belt. (Youens/Osprey)

By the end of the Peninsular War blue-grey trousers had replaced the white for other ranks. The private's regiment is shown by the buff-coloured facings. (Youens/Osprey)

81

booty. Such was the result of Wellesley's first great victory and the ensuing Convention of Cintra.

When Sir John Moore set off into Spain with two-thirds of the army he had in Portugal, the Buffs were assigned escort duties. This involved wide dispersal and much toil in pushing baggage-carts through the winter mud; consequently only the Grenadier Company could join up with Moore when he was compelled to retreat on Corunna. They fought with the rearguard and were evacuated in a ragged and emaciated state, while the remainder of the battalion contrived to make a safe return to Portugal.

Sir Arthur Wellesley, having been recalled to England for an inquiry, returned to Portugal in April 1809 and lost no time in striking out northwards to gain Oporto. The Buffs led the advance and were the first to reach the River Douro, just after the bridge into Oporto had been blown up in the early hours of 12 May.

Out of a British total of 121 casualties the Buffs suffered fifty, and they received full credit in Wellesley's despatch. In September 1813 they and three other regiments were awarded the honour of 'Douro', to be borne on their regimental colour. This was a new way of commemorating a famous victory, and ten years were to elapse before the Buffs were to receive similar awards for other battles of the Peninsula.

Their next battle was Talavera, fought on 27 July 1809. They were in Rowland Hill's 2nd Division, holding the heights on the extreme left, and it was here that the French made their main attack, with massive support from their cannon. Ordered by Wellesley to lie down beyond the brow, the six battalions waited there for the great columns of Frenchmen to reach the summit, then shattered them with their volleys and chased them back down the hill. The Buffs had 152 casualties, with their commanding officer among the dead.

Lord Wellington (raised to the peerage for this victory), was now forced to make a gradual retreat to the Lines of Torres Vedras. The 2nd Division had no real fighting either in the retreat or in the repulse of the enemy from these lines, and it was then detached under General Beresford on flank-protection duties, which unexpectedly involved the siege of the recently-fallen Badajoz. While still in the early stages of the siege, Beresford heard that Soult was marching on him from the south, and he rushed his hetero-genous force to the village of La Albuhera and the ridge above it. This was on 15 May 1811; the 16th was the most horrific in the Buff's history.

Early on this morning the Buffs were sent down the ridge to La Albuhera and were then rushed back up the hill to contend with the massive attack that was coming in round the right flank and throwing the Spaniards into confusion. The Buffs were halted on the Spaniards' right and at once suffered losses from cannon shot. They were then thrown into the attack, and, after firing two volleys, they saw the French break before them as they advanced far ahead of the remainder of the brigade. Then down came a blinding hailstorm, and through it two regiments of cavalry – French hussars and Polish lancers – swept in among the Buffs from their right rear.

Around 400 Buffs were spiked or hacked down in a matter of minutes, and when the roll was called after the battle only eighty-five were left to answer out of 728. The colours were defended with especial heroism.

After hours of fighting, this disastrous opening was redeemed by a charge of the Fusilier Brigade, which drove the French from the hill and regained the Buffs' Regimental colour (starting an enduring friendship between the Buffs and the Royal Fusiliers).

So quickly were the ranks of the Buffs refilled that they gained the nickname of 'Resurrectionists'. During the next eighteen months they had some exhausting marches, sometimes advancing, some-times retreating, but fought no pitched battle until Wellington began his final advance on France in the summer of 1813. At Vitoria they gained a battle honour without being closely engaged. In the Pyrenees they were on outpost duty when Soult struck with overwhelming force and they played a crucial part in drawing the sting from his advance, which nevertheless brought Wellington's generals to the verge of panic before he could intervene in person and send Soult's thousands rolling back into France. On 10 November the Buffs were to the fore with the 2nd Division when Wellington made entry into France by ripping apart the defences beyond the Nivelle, and on 13 December they held the extreme right of the line beyond the swollen Nive when Soult again attacked with what should have been overwhelming force. Here the Buffs brilliantly redeemed a withdrawal ordered by their commanding officer. When it was countermanded by the brigade commander, Sir John

Byng, the men turned about with a great cheer and drove back the massed, overconfident Frenchmen with devastating courage.

They subsequently played minor parts in the reduction of Orthez and Toulouse, and in June 1814, within a mere three months of completing their five-and-a-half years of continuous campaigning, they were shipped to Canada to wage war against the United States.

Uniforms

In America, the peculiarities of some officers' dress sanctioned in the Peninsula were noted with disfavour, and among the items that appear to have been unofficially discarded are the cocked hat and the silver epaulette, which could make an officer look both conspicuous and ridiculous. The soldiers who had worn the stovepipe hat around 1811 exchanged it for the Wellington shako. Around the same time the breeches and leggings gave way to blue-grey trousers. It would appear that officers also donned shakos and trousers, no doubt adding their individual eccentricities. The troops had never been less ornate and were frequently shabby. They were also victorious.

Since 1770 the old three-cornered hat had been taking a new shape. By 1790 the back and front peaks were turned up so high that they had to be laced into position. The black feathers were purchased at the men's own expense, and, according to an Inspection Report of 1791, cost 'from 10 pence to one shilling each'. Officers' hats were bound with silver tape, whereas those of the men were bound in white. The uniform of officers and men differed very little: a scarlet coat cut back like morning dress and fastened with silver or white metal buttons; buff facings, cuffs and waistcoat, and breeches worn with black gaiters and shoes. In the case of an officer, all lace on the coat was silver, and his rank was further denoted by the wearing of a single silver epaulette, a silver gorget – worn on duty – and a crimson sash around the waist. All officers carried a sword and the sword-belt appears to have changed from buff leather to white since the Warrant of 1768. The white metal belt-plate carries the regimental number and motto, '*Veteri frondescit honore*'.

From 1796 to 1802 a number of changes in the dress of the infantry soldier took place. In 1803 the infantry coat of NCOs and men of the Buffs had become a single-breasted coatee with short tails, cut to the waist

in front and the the seat behind, with high buff collar, cuffs, and bars of buff across the front. Breeches and gaiters continued to be the general form of dress, though tight-fitting pantaloons were sometimes worn. On 24 February 1800 the wearing of the peaked stovepipe hat, copied from the Austrian Infantry, was authorized; only officers continued to wear the cocked hat.

While other ranks wore the short coatee, officers, when in full dress or off duty, retained the uniform coat with long tails. The coatee as worn by NCOs and men was worn only when the officer was on duty. Officers also retained their cocked hats, and these were now worn crosswise. White breeches and knee-boots were worn in normal dress, as well as white or blue pantaloons with Hessian boots, while on ceremonial occasions an officer would wear white breeches with black gaiters.

There is little difference between the private's and the officer's uniform of the same period, except that the private's coat possibly would have been of poorer quality cloth. His hat was edged with white tape in place of silver, and, similarly, instead of silver lacing on his coat, the regimental yellow, black, and crimson lace appeared. Neither gorget, sash, nor epaulette were worn, of course, and cross-belts replaced the officers' single sword-belt.

By 1814 blue-grey trousers were the standard issue for the men. The red, single-breasted coat with regimental lace, buff collar and cuffs, and white crossbelts was still worn. Up to 1800 the greatcoat was not a general issue, but after the campaign in Holland in 1806 it was decided that all NCOs and men should be provided with a greatcoat of a stout grey material, fitted with a cape. This can be seen rolled on top of the pack of a private of 1814, and fastened with white tape. The stovepipe-pattern headdress worn by the men was so similar to that worn by the French that, in order to avoid confusion in battle, it was changed to the Wellington shako in about 1811.

The Argyll and Sutherland Highlanders
The Argyllshire Highlanders
The 98th Highlanders arrived in Simonstown in September 1795, as part of a force some 4,500 strong under Sir Alured Clarke, an ambitious officer for whom the conquest of the Dutch colony at the Cape was the one great chance of achieving military renown. But his second-in-command had already

Painting of the founder of the 93rd (Argyll and Sutherland Highlanders) wearing its original uniform. Note the heavy half-plaid over his shoulder.

The uniform of the 3rd Sutherland Fencibles (becoming part of the Argyll and Sutherland Highlanders in 1798) is here worn by a famous regimental character – Sergeant Samuel ('Big Sam') Macdonald.

forced a landing with the advance guard, and had driven the Dutch off their only tenable defensive position in front of Cape Town. When Sir Alured faced the vastly outnumbered Dutch at Wynberg, they cheated him of his great victory by running away after one ragged volley which cost his army one seaman killed and seventeen soldiers wounded, four of them from the 98th. So the 98th had, technically, their baptism of fire, and settled down as the permanent garrison, to suffer for seven unhappy years really serious casualties from the insalubrious climate and the insanitary conditions in Cape Castle. They lost eleven dead in the first month; and they seldom had less than 100 sick in hospital.

Much worse, however, for morale was the order in

December to adopt the standard uniform of the British Army in India. Lochnell, the Commanding Officer, had been at vast trouble to fit them all out with six yards each of the dark green Campbell tartan with the black stripe. For the rest they wore the full Highland dress: scarlet coats faced with yellow for both officers and men; black stocks, leather for rank and file, velvet for the officers; diced hose in red and white with scarlet garters, and Highland shoes with yellow or gold oval shoe-buckles. Lace with black and white cotton for NCOs and men, silver for officers; and officers' epaulettes, when worn, were also of silver lace. All ranks wore the regulation Highland feather bonnet, and officers wore their own hair, clubbed over the ears with red rosettes on each club, and the

The private in the 93rd Highlanders wears the uniform used in South Africa; no concession was made to the heat. Note the lambswool tufts worn in place of epaulettes by battalion companies only. (Roffe/Osprey)

The officer wears the uniform in which the Argyll and Sutherland Highlanders were first raised and which is similar to that of other Scottish regiments. In 1804 the silver epaulettes were replaced by gold. (Roffe/Osprey)

The short hair of the officer follows the fashion begun in about 1808. The kilt of the 91st Argyllshire Highlanders worn here scarcely differs from that of the 93rd. (Roffe/Osprey)

85

queue tied with a black bow. All this had now to be abandoned for garments no more suitable for hot climates than the kilt, and drearily undistinguished: white trousers with black half-gaiters, scarlet tunics and absurd round, black, felt hats, 'at least 6 inches high with a 4-inch brim', curled up at the sides, with a plume over the left ear, white for the grenadier company, green for the light company and black for battalion companies. The troops stagnated and went down in large numbers with various local diseases. There was a brief flutter of military activity when the Dutch attempted to recover their colony in 1796. But their Admiral, faced with overwhelming military force on land and blockaded by a superior fleet at sea, surrendered without landing a man or firing a shot.

Now renumbered 91st, the regiment, under the terms of the Treaty of Amiens, handed Cape Colony back to the Dutch and reassembled at Bexhill in May 1803. They were much depleted in numbers, having been heavily milked in their last months at the Cape to bring the regiments destined for India up to full strength; and it took them more then a year to get back their full Highland dress. From 1804 onwards the men were issued with six yards of tartan every two years for the upkeep of their kilts. All ranks wore the Kilmarnock bonnet, cocked, for fatigues and minor parades, covering it with the feather bonnet for ceremonial occasions. The plaid became increasingly a purely ceremonial garment, and officers were forbidden the kilt as ball and dinner dress. To compensate, they were allowed gold epaulettes instead of silver.

All this helped to keep up morale for another five years of inactive soldiering, moving about southern England as part of the forces hopefully gathered to defeat Napoleon if the admirals ever let him slip across the Channel. They had a brief hope of better things when the Highland Brigade was sent to Hanover at the end of 1805. But they were back in Kent throughout 1806, and thereafter in Cork. Throughout all this they clearly remained a very good regiment. Nevertheless, the campaign was as disappointing for the 91st as it was for the nation as a whole. The light company of the 91st was engaged at Roliça and had a sergeant severely wounded. But the regiment as a whole was in reserve and was not

Four different shoulder-belt plates from regiments that became part of the 93rd (Argyll and Sutherland Highlanders).

Three men from different walks of life meet on the way to enlist for the Argylls; recruits included fishermen, crofters, and sons of wealthy farmers.

The 93rd (Argyll and Sutherland Highlanders) are here seen preparing food during their expedition to Cape Town. Note the white 'shell' jackets and 'Kilmarnock bonnets'.

Highland regiment, and it was from the office of the Adjutant-General, whose clerks had for over 200 years put their own convenience before the interests of the fighting soldier, that the blow fell. Recruiting difficulties and the allegation that their national dress was 'objectionable to the natives of South Britain' were made the excuse for striking six regiments off the Highland establishment, though in fact the 91st enlisted in all, between 1800 and 1818, 970 Scots as against 171 Englishmen, 218 Irishmen, and twenty-two foreigners, mostly Germans. Moreover, from 1807 to 1814 their 2nd Battalion recruited 599 Scots, 168 Englishmen, 142 Irishmen, and 197 foreigners. Since the tartan had already been issued for new kilts, the 91st found some consolation in having it made up into trews; and they adopted a flat, black bonnet ornamented with a single feather. This was the uniform in which they were dispatched on the Walcheren expedition.

The devastating low fever peculiar to the island of Walcheren had already destroyed one British army 200 years before. This time, from 3 September to 23 December, an army of 40,000 men lay encamped there because the generals could not agree on what to do with them. During these four months no less than 35,000 of them passed through the military hospitals to a precarious convalescence or the grave. By 25 September, after only three weeks, the 91st had only 246 rank and file fit for duty out of 608. From disease the regiment lost a total of 218 dead – far more than all their casualties in the Corunna campaign. During the six months following their return to Kent they had an average of 250 sick, and it was quite impossible to train or drill them to any acceptable standard. On top of this they were deprived of even their trews and

engaged in either of the major battles. It was again in the reserve division for Sir John Moore's spectacular march to Salamanca which disrupted Napoleon's whole campaign; and it came into its own at last when the reserve division became the rearguard for the epic retreat which culminated in Moore's victory and death at Corunna. The 91st had then more than their fair share of privations and forced marches; and in the rearguard actions in which they were engaged they lost 164 of all ranks killed, wounded, or missing. At Corunna itself, though 'in the very centre of the line and next the Guards', they were not heavily engaged and lost only two men wounded. 'Corunna', nevertheless, was a worthily won battle honour to be placed on the Colours beside 'Roliça' and 'Vimeiro'.

But for the 91st the rest of the year 1809 was disastrous. They lost their kilt and their status as a

Three items of officer's equipment worn for the latter half of the Napoleonic Wars: cap badge for Kilmarnock bonnet; bonnet badge; crossbelt buckle.

bonnets. Henceforth they wore the blue-grey trousers and black cap of an English line regiment: a uniform in which few of the troops and none of the officers took the smallest pride. All that remained of their origin was the Pipe Band and the title of His Majesty's 91st Argyllshire Regiment.

As such, they rejoined Wellington in 1812. They missed Vitoria; but with the 6th Division at Sorauren on 28 and 30 July 1813, in what Wellington called 'bludgeon work', they played a decisive part in dislodging Marshal Soult from the positions he had hoped to hold in the Pyrenees. On the first day the 91st suffered heavily, losing 115 killed and wounded out of a total strength of 821. On the second day, when the brigaded light companies bore the brunt, they got off lightly. But they clearly played their full part in what even Wellington called 'desperate fighting', adding that he had 'never known the troops behave so well'. 'Pyrenees' was another battle honour on the 91st Colours which was well and truly earned.

The back view of this 93rd Highlander officer shows the way the half-plaid was attached by a rosette after the Peninsular War. The ornamented coat-tails (skirts) can also be seen. (Roffe/Osprey)

The officer of the 91st Argyllshire Highlanders wears the half-plaid that was, in 1808, a recent introduction. Here it is worn over the shoulder and freed at the back, in contrast to the later style using the rosette. (Roffe/Osprey)

They were to win four more in France: 'Nivelle', 'Nive', 'Orthez', 'Toulouse', with 'Peninsular' thrown in as a general makeweight. The first three were not costly, and the only distinction was the promotion in the field of the Adjutant, Lieutenant MacNeil of Colonsay, after he had had two horses killed under him at the passage of the Nive.

At Toulouse, on 10 April 1814, Soult put up a last, desperate fight, which cost Wellington close on 5,000 casualties. Sir Denis Pack's Highland Brigade led the 6th Division attack brilliantly, ending up with the 42nd and 78th holding three captured enemy redoubts, and the 91st in close support behind. When a French column, 6,000 strong, counterattacked, the 42nd were driven back in some disorder, but the prompt support of the 91st gave them time to re-form; and the two battalions together then success-fully restored the position. By the time the 91st got back to their position the other wing was in trouble; once more they sallied out, again completely restored the position, and rescued a large party of the 78th who had been surrounded and were in danger of being made prisoner. Every general present reckoned that only the vigorous support afforded by the Argyllshire regiment had saved the Brigade at a very critical moment in the battle. So the war ended for the 91st in a blaze of glory, with nine battle honours on the Regimental Colour. But at Waterloo they were left far on the right flank; and, though they got the campaign medal, that great battle was never in-scribed on their Colours. One more fragment of military glory nevertheless came their way. The 2nd Battalion, raised purely as a feeder for the 1st, was a pretty motley crew. At their annual inspection in 1809 the older men were still wearing out their forbidden kilts, the rest were wearing 'pantaloons, breeches, or trews', and they could muster only 130 all ranks. But their acquisition three years later of a dynamic Commanding Officer, Lieutenant-Colonel Ottley, some able lieutenants and 309 disbanded militiamen, encouraged the War Department to bring them up to full strength with all sorts of 'undesirables' – 'old, worn-out men', 'an inferior type of boy', and some displaced Swedes, Pomeranians, and Hanoverians – and send them to the Baltic. They saw their first and last action at the disastrous night attack on the fortress of Bergen-op-Zoom in 1814, and thanks to Ottley's training did very well. All four of the assaulting columns successfully stormed the

A sergeant of the 93rd Highlanders, with his half-pike at his side, dressed in the trews worn for the New Orleans campaign in 1814. He wears the Kilmarnock bonnet; his hackle is replaced by a white 'tourie'. (Roffe/Osprey)

outer walls, only to be thrown back by superior numbers of veteran French troops manning the inner defences. The Battalion withdrew in admirable order, leaving thirteen officers and an unrecorded number of men wounded, and losing altogether forty-five killed or mortally wounded. So far as is known, the Surgeon and Assistant Surgeon were the only unwounded to fall into enemy hands; and Sergeant-Major Cahill was commissioned in the field for saving the Regimental Colour when the ensign carrying it went down. So, having unexpectedly found a niche in military history, the 2nd Battalion came home to be disbanded after sending 240 men to the 1st Battalion for the Waterloo campaign.

The 93rd (Sutherland Highlanders)

Unlike the 91st, the 93rd had from 1800 to 1815 a relatively stable and peaceful existence. They were brought back from Guernsey after two years and in February 1803 they were sent to quell a brief recrudescence of rebellion in Dublin. They spent one fortnight aboard ship under orders, fortunately cancelled, for Jamaica. Instead they sailed, in July 1805, to recapture Cape Colony; there, like the 91st, they had their baptism of fire and won their first – for many years their only – battle honour.

The Dutch were better prepared this time. General Janssen had nearly 2,000 regular infantry, a squadron of dragoons, and sixteen guns served by a mixed crew of Europeans, Javanese and black slaves from Mozambique. He had hoped for a substantial reinforcement of mounted burghers, but the harvest kept all but 224 at home. Major-General Sir David Baird had on his transports three times Janssen's numbers; but he had to get them and their guns ashore on open beaches through a heavy surf and prevent their dying from thirst and heat-exhaustion on the inevitably long approach march. His first attempted landing, on 5 January 1806, was foiled by the surf, and he therefore sent an infantry regiment and his cavalry to secure a comparatively easy landing miles away, in case he should have to take the whole force round and accept the appalling administrative problem of supplying it for several days in a waterless desert before he could make contact with his enemy. Actually he got his force ashore the next day for the loss of only thirty-seven of the 93rd, and made a good fight of it. Baird, by detaching a whole brigade to hold off what turned out to be only a handful of

mounted burghers on his flank, had only half his available force, his Highland Brigade, to face the whole Dutch Army; and on the field, infantry and guns were pretty evenly matched. The Highlanders fought without subtlety, merely deploying into line and, after a preliminary discharge of artillery, advancing with fixed bayonets and the pipers in front, pausing to fire one volley at an extreme range, and then charging home. With the 93rd, young, enthusiastic and wholly inexperienced, in the centre of the line, it was probably the best way. Two-thirds of the 5th Waldeck Regiment left the field when the guns opened, though Janssen himself knocked the major in command down and shot one fugitive with his pistol. His rage inspired the rest of his troops to make a stout fight of it; and when he drew off in good order he left 400 killed and wounded and had inflicted some 200 casualties on the Scots. The 93rd lost five officers wounded and two men killed; but forty-two out of their fifty-three wounded died of their wounds.

This virtually ended the campaign. Cape Town was surrendered; and seven of the disgraced Waldeck officers and twenty of their troopers committed suicide. Janssen tried himself to hold out for ten days in the mountains, finally surrendering his remaining 1,050 men, and with them Cape Colony, on 18 January. The surviving Waldeckers cheerfully accepted 20 dollars each to join the British Army; and the 93rd moved into the old home of the 91st in Cape Castle, where they remained for the next eight years.

Uniforms

The so-called 'little kilt' had by 1800 replaced the old single garment, the belted plaid, but the decorative plaid worn over the left shoulder as a vestigial remnant of the old garment had not yet been sanctioned. The officer's double-breasted jacket was buttoned to the neck, as for action or field training. For more formal occasions the top two buttons would be undone and buttoned back to form two yellow-faced lapels. This facing ran down to the bottom of the coat on both sides. For full, or ball, dress the facings would be completely buttoned back and hooked together down the middle to make a plastron of yellow, laced with silver. The silver epaulettes were to be replaced by gold throughout the Highland Brigade in 1804.

The 93rd first went into action at the Cape, with

galoshes over pewter-buckled shoes and black gaiters worn by all non-commissioned ranks. The coat of the private was single-breasted and the crossbelt buckle a different shape from the officer's and of bronze picked out with brass, instead of silver and gilt; and his buttons were pewter instead of silver. But, like his officer, he did not turn down the hose over his garters – a custom unique to the 93rd.

The uniform worn by officers of the 91st during the first fifteen years of the regiment's existence, before it lost its Highland status and accoutrements altogether, conformed much more strictly to the Dress Regulations for His Majesty's Highland Regiments than did the 93rd. They always wore, for example, a white edging of false collar round the inside of the black stock. The plain, steel-hilted broadsword, without regimental insignia, was the standard pattern for the Highland Brigade. They turned their hose down over their garters, and they wore no foxtails on their feathered bonnets. The sporran, also, conformed exactly to the standard pattern: so that on one occasion, when Lochnell had ordered too many, he was able to sell off the surplus to another regiment. The tartan is that described by Lochnell in his letter to the Duke of Argyll – the dark green Campbell, with the black line, which was in fact almost indistinguish-

Painting of the battle of Alexandria. Private Lutz of the Queen's Own (96th) Regiment is shown bringing the French standard he had captured to General Abercromby. (National Army Museum)

able from the Sutherland. The gorget, too, was worn, correctly, suspended from a yellow ribbon round the neck, and not hung, as in the 93rd, from two small gold buttons.

At Christmas, 1804, full Highland dress was restored to the 91st in place of the detested Cape uniform. But Dress Regulations for Highland regiments had changed since 1795. Officers wore full Highland dress for all duties, but off duty changed to white breeches and Hessian boots. Field and staff officers wore breeches and half-boots at all times, and carried a sabre instead of the broadsword. The 93rd, always wayward in such matters, appear to have ignored these regulations. The 91st were more conformist in every particular. The coat and bonnet, the tartan silk waist and shoulder sashes, with the narrow crimson stripe over the shoulder, were standard wear for all Highland field officers. The recently introduced half-plaid was slung from the left shoulder and hitched to the belt at the back, under the coat.

The King's Regiment and the Queen's Own
The King's were greatly involved in the West Indies. The Grenadier and Light Companies formed part of a force under General Grey that re-captured Martinique and Guadeloupe in 1794. The following year the whole Regiment sailed for the West Indies. Owing to storms, only four companies arrived to assist in the capture of St Lucia and the suppression of a

The officer of the 8th or King's Regiment shows through his unbuttoned coat the frill of his shirt above the gold gorget and his white waistcoat below. The six buttons of the gaiters are of bone. (Roffe/Osprey)

The long coat of the private in the 63rd regiment was to be replaced before the turn of the century. Note that the Brown Bess's triangular bayonet does not obstruct the barrel. (Roffe/Osprey)

rebellion in Grenada. Later in 1809 both the 8th and 63rd, from Nova Scotia and Barbados respectively, took part in yet another assault on Martinique and this battle honour is the first shared by both regiments. The 63rd remained in the West Indies for nearly twelve years and, in a well organized nine day campaign with light casualties, won a further battle honour, 'Guadeloupe 1810'. While losses from enemy action were negligible, disease and the dreaded fever took a heavy toll. In 1815, for instance, the Regiment

was at half strength and still had to find no less than ten detachments on other islands. When the Regiment sailed for England in 1819 it left behind the scattered graves of nearly 1,500 officers and men. Of the first sixty-two years of its separate existence the 63rd had served fifty-five overseas, of which thirty-one had been spent in North America and the West Indies.

The Queen's Own, 96th of Foot
From the beginning of the Seven Years War, right

The blue facings seen here on the collar and cuffs were awarded at the end of the Peninsular War when the regiment became the 96th Queen's Own (Royal) Regiment. The officer is also wearing the new blue-grey trousers. (Roffe/Osprey)

Charles Stuart captured Minorca in 1798 he found among the prisoners over a thousand Swiss who had been captured in Italy and sold to the Spaniards for two dollars a head. With a leavening of English officers, these Swiss were formed into a regiment to fight once more against the French and two years later, as the Minorca Regiment, they accompanied General Abercromby's expedition to Egypt.

The decisive battle of Alexandria took place on the narrow peninsula three miles east of the city. In it, the Minorca Regiment, which was part of a reserve brigade commanded by Brigadier Stuart, taking up a position between the Guards' Brigade and the fort, won lasting renown by destroying the French dragoons as they made their last desperate charge.

In addition a Private Lutz of the regiment gained himself a gratuity and a pension of £20 a year for the rest of his life when he regained a French standard originally captured by the 42nd only to be snatched back by a French officer. He was presented with a finely-worked miniature of the trophy to wear on his uniform and an order was issued that a 'valuable badge' should be instituted for those of his comrades who had 'distinguished themselves by acts of valour or by personal instances of meritorious service'.

On the Regiment's arrival in England it was brought into the line as the 97th. Between 1808 and 1811 the Regiment served with distinction under Wellington in the Peninsular Army, but the casualties were such that it had to be sent to England to re-form. Here a further honour awaited the survivors. They now proudly wore the blue facings of a Royal Regiment and as 'The Queen's Own' served in Canada on the Niagara frontier alongside the King's. Shortly before the Regiment was disbanded in 1818, the 96th was taken out of the line and the Queen's Own took over their number. Only five years later regiments numbered 94 to 99 were re-formed.

Uniforms

The uniforms of the 63rd and The Queen's Own were similar to other infantry regiments, and require no special comment. For the private of a line company of the 63rd the dark green regimental facings on the coat from the collar to waist were 3 inches wide, with ten white loops. The buttons were of embossed white metal. The white duck trousers buttoned on the outside of the knee with four white bone buttons (also used on gaiters). The brass crossbelt plate has '63'

through to 1815, there were constant demands for more and more troops to serve overseas. Over these sixty years no less than four regiments numbered '96th' were raised and dispatched to overseas stations, as far apart as India and the West Indies. Then, when the crisis seemed to have passed, it was their fate to be 'reduced', shipped home, and disbanded. Yet another regiment in its closing years was numbered '96th' and bequeathed its battle honours to the last British regiment to bear this number. When Brigadier

within the Garter and Crown.

For the 96th Queen's Own (Royal) Regiment blue facings and silver lace were authorized when the Regiment received its new title during the Peninsular War. The capture of the 'Invincibles' standard was commemorated on the buttons, crossbelt and shako plate, on all of which appeared a Sphinx with a French flag over the left shoulder. The shako plate was silver, mounted on gold lace with a crimson line.

The Royal Artillery

When Revolutionary France invaded the Netherlands in 1793, the Duke of York took an army to Flanders in which the artillery was under the command of Major (later Sir William) Congreve. The guns were actually attached directly to the infantry battalions and not organized as an artillery brigade, but at the siege of Valenciennes it was realized that guns were needed to fire in battery and they were thus detached from the infantry. After two months' bombardment the garrison surrendered. Although the campaign had some success for the British troops, an engagement with the French army in May brought defeat and the expedition returned home early in 1794.

In 1799 another large expedition consisting of companies of artillery and a troop of horse artillery went to the Helder in North Holland where it met a Russian force, and both combined under the command of the Duke of York. This was the first occasion that the new body of horse artillery formed in 1793 went into action. Artillery guns had some success against the French dragoons, but no useful conclusion came from the expedition. The Royal Artillery was now organized into brigades and no longer attached to infantry battalions.

The French had been established in Egypt since 1799 and so a British expedition set sail in the Mediterranean. Under strong fire the troops landed at Aboukir in 1801, the artillery getting its field pieces ashore at the same time as the infantry. The heavy artillery then bombarded the castle of Aboukir which surrendered a few days later. There were thirty-four pieces available for use at the subsequent Battle of Alexandria, but being without means of draught these were not used. Had horses been available it is possible that the fate of Alexandria would have been decided that day.

By August two batteries had been established, but not before some strenuous manhandling of the guns over most difficult rocks and countryside. The only horses which could have been made available were the offcasts of the weakened cavalry. Once the guns were in position the bombardment was successful and Alexandria had to surrender. Elsewhere in Egypt the British forces defeated the French and remained there until the Peace of Amiens in March 1802. All those participants in this campaign were thereafter personally allowed to wear a special badge commemorating Egypt, the first time that such a distinction had been granted to all ranks in the British forces. The badge of a sphinx was worn on the soldier's headdress, and retained even if he should join another unit. Officers of artillery carried the sphinx on the sabretache while other officers in the battalion or troop did not. The honour title of 'Sphinx' is borne by five batteries in modern times.

On the gilt belt-plate can be seen the badge of three cannons on a shield underneath a crown. The belt-plate is of the Sandwich Volunteer Artillery in about 1806.

When the French troops were driven out of the West Indies, many small though important actions took place, especially Martinique in 1809. Fort Royal had fallen but Fort Desaix was a strongpoint defended by 120 artillery pieces. Gunners and sailors worked day and night for ten days in pouring rain to establish five batteries. A continuous bombardment achieved its aim when the main enemy magazine was blown up by a mortar shell on 24 February. For its stout work in the attack Captain Stewart's company was allowed a choice of trophies. It is said that, as the men knew they were soon due for transfer to a new situation, a beautiful brass one-pounder French gun had to be refused, and in its place a French pioneer's axe and a brass drum were chosen. The drum has disappeared, but the axe with the badge of an eagle attached is carried by the tallest gunner when 'Battle Axe' day is celebrated in the battery on 24 February each year. The battery is sometimes called the 'Battle Axe' Company. As this company is descended from one of the companies of the old Royal Irish Artillery, one wonders whether its members had remembered that the old galloglasses of ancient Ireland survived as the Battle Axe Guards in the late seventeenth century and took this evocative title.

At the start of the Peninsular War a British army complete with artillery sailed to Portugal. At first, the two artillery companies were under the command of Colonel Robe. In August, General Wellesley, later the Duke of Wellington, attacked Roliça and there a battery used shrapnel for the first time in action and to good effect. Captain Shrapnel of the Royal Artillery later received a handsome pension for his invention. Later, at Vimiero, the discharge of spherical case (the early name for shrapnel) from the nine-pounder batteries drew off the menacing French cavalry. In an evening battle when the French infantry nearly overwhelmed the British, a delayed and well-timed volley at sixty yards broke the attacking column and the 50th Foot chased the retreating enemy for nearly 300 yards.

Sir John Moore and a new army brought 712 fresh artillerymen from England, but several died during the difficult landing. The French under Napoleon forced their retreat, and in January 1809 the Emperor felt confident enough to hand over to Marshal Soult. Moore decided to use Corunna as his base for withdrawal. The artillery beat off the French attack and successfully covered the retreat.

The following year Wellesley returned to Portugal to force the French out of that country. Within a few days the French were driven out of Oporto. At the Battle of Talavera in July 1809 neither horses nor mules could be found to draw the field guns. However the best was done and British, Spanish, and Portuguese batteries fought together in this battle. The approach of a French army in his rear caused Wellington to retire, but one of the three British batteries earned the honour title of 'Talavera'.

Having occupied most of Spain, in late 1809 and the following spring the French army made ready to drive the British out of Portugal. At Busaco in

This print by J. A. Atkinson of artillerymen shows the uniforms of 1807. The hair tied in a queue can be seen here beneath the stovepipe shakos. Beside the cannon are a number of cannon-balls and a ramrod.

September a stand was made. The horse artillery rendered great service, and, after the artillery caused heavy losses, the French withdrew. Lord Wellington now returned to his strongly fortified lines at Torres Vedras.

At La Albuhera in May 1811 the British artillery and that of the King's German Legion were hotly engaged, the latter being somewhat cut up during a ferocious charge by the famous Polish Lancers.

A siege train was formed to take Ciudad Rodrigo, which fell in January 1812 after 200 rounds per gun had been fired. Badajoz was the next to fall to the bombardment of the siege train. Wellington was now able to undertake operations in the field in which Portuguese artillery accompanied the British. At Salamanca a breach was not initially effected as supplies of ammunition had become exhausted, but

The gunner's uniform in 1792 has the long coat and bicorn hat. Over the pack can be seen the powder-horn; the priming wires and spiking-hammer are on the shoulder-belt. (Roffe/Osprey)

The gunner with the long queue tied tightly over his back, is wearing blue pantaloons with short gaiters, an alternative in the early 1800s to white breeches. Overalls were not yet generally worn. (Roffe/Osprey)

in July the battle was successfully engaged. The winter of 1812–13 was spent in reorganizing, and reinforcements were found for the artillery.

In April 1813 four mountain guns under Captain

Arabin engaged the enemy at Bier. By June, Joseph Bonaparte had his soldiers in front of Vitoria, and his artillery checked the advance of the 3rd, 4th, and 7th Divisions. The British artillery joined the conflict, and after half an hour so weakened the enemy that a general advance was made possible in which the heights were carried and twenty-eight pieces of artillery captured. The final victory saw 150 cannon abandoned on the field of battle. Wellington's report to the Prince Regent was sufficient to bring a special cash award to all the officers commanding artillery.

The French army was now hard pressed. At San Sebastian a three-month siege with fifty-nine pieces of heavy ordnance softening the fortress led to victory by assault. The storming parties were astonished to hear artillery firing in their rear, for this was the first occasion that infantry was supported by artillery bombardment over their heads. By five o'clock in the evening of 31 August 1813 San Sebastian was in the hands of the British.

In pursuing the French troops across the Pyrenees, the use of mountain artillery was effected by Lieutenant Robe who instigated the carrying of three-pounder guns on mules. In November the Battle of Nivelle was fought and the Allies entered France. The artillery continued in the advance across France and was present at the crossing of the River Adour, and at the sieges of Bayonne, St Étienne, Aire, and Toulouse. By 1814 Napoleon realized his impossible position and abdicated.

The Peninsula was not the only battlefield of this period. After extensive preparations the Americans declared war on Great Britain in 1812. The British achieved a victory at the Battle of Queenstown, but at the cost of the life of the commander of the British forces, General Brock. At Fort Erie in November the militia artillery was surprised and routed; gunboats were engaged in minor actions; artillery under Captain Jackson took part in the action at Chrysler's Farm, and later on their retreat Fort Niagara was captured. For their action in Canada some artillerymen were allowed to wear the word 'Niagara' on their appointments, and later a battery was given this as an honour title.

In 1814 fresh troops were sent to America. An attack on the American capital was planned. In August the Battle of Bladensburg saw British rockets successfully in action, and soon after this government buildings in Washington, including the Capitol, the Arsenal, and the Dockyard, were set on fire; 194 cannon were captured on this occasion. At Baltimore in September, where General Ross, commander of the British forces, was killed, the British artillery did great execution and created a panic which brought

This officer of the Gunners is wearing the 1793 style of overseas service uniform. His headdress is peculiar; it is made of felt with a plume to give it a military appearance. (Roffe/Osprey)

about the defeat of the American forces. But in the new year at the Battle of New Orleans it was the British who suffered defeat, this unfortunate battle taking place a week after peace had been concluded.

When Napoleon came out of exile in February 1815, artillerymen from Britain and America went to the Netherlands to build up the Allied armies which were assembling to counter the French threat. Sir George Adam Wood was made commander of the artillery on the Continent. In the battle ranks were six troops of Royal Horse Artillery with the cavalry, and two in reserve, while eight companies or batteries of Royal Artillery as well as others in reserve were ready for general use. Most batteries were formed into brigades of five nine-pounders and one $5\frac{1}{2}$-inch howitzer.

At Quatre Bras the day before Waterloo only two field batteries were engaged, with losses of nine men killed and one of the majors slightly wounded. At Waterloo, Wellington had the artillery on the crest of rising ground with the infantry just below it, and the cavalry to the left, and behind the centre. When the French cavalry attacked, the guns fired to the last moment and then retired into the infantry squares, none of which were broken. When some guns of the King's German Legion were overrun by cavalry the gunners defended themselves with their heavy brass-hilted swords. At the end of the day when the Old Guard made three attacks on Wellington's front, the cannon duel was terrific. The allied artillery kept up its fire on the Guard, but when they ignored it and reached the top of the crest Wellington gave the order for the British to advance and the day was won. Although Napoleon was defeated, the Royal Artillery had to reduce the minor fortresses still resisting on the frontiers until all had surrendered.

Waterloo was regarded as a special distinction for all those serving in this battle, and for the first time every man was given a medal. 'Waterloo' was an honour to be worn on artillery distinctions, but in 1833 it was decided that as artillery had served in so many theatres of war there was little purpose in awarding separate honours. The Royal Regiment of Artillery was now awarded '*Ubique*' meaning 'Everywhere', and '*Quo Fas et Gloria Ducunt*', 'Where Right and Glory lead'. The grant of the Royal Arms above a gun accompanied this award.

Uniforms
Towards the end of the eighteenth century military dress was very stylish. The gunner's hat became so cocked that it was almost a bicorn and it carried a plume, a fashion which gained popularity during the American Revolution.

The coat was close-fitting and the sewn-down skirts could never be loosened. The collar was of the 'stand-up' variety and the buttonhole connected with the top hole on the lapel. The pouch-belt had the Royal

Crown and a scroll on the flap, which usually bore the battalion number. On top of the pouch was the small powder-horn used for priming. On the chest, in white leather holders, were two priming-wires to pierce the cartridge and the brass-headed hammer used to spike the touch-hole of cannon.

The hair at this time was elaborately prepared. It was brushed into a plait at the back and held in place with a strap. After a long and tedious process, grease and powder produced the white appearance. The elaborate ruffle on the chest developed from the shirt frill, and although elegant for a parade was of little use to a fighting man.

The top-hat, sometimes worn, was a popular civilian headdress. Being less cumbersome than the cocked hat it was provided for troops on overseas service. Suitable extras like yellow braid and a red feather in front made it more military.

Although overalls were not common issue until the next century, loose trousers were more serviceable on active duties then the tight gaiters and white breeches. The hair was still curled at the sides and brought to a queue at the back and tied with ribbon, but mercifully greasing and powdering was being discontinued.

The gunner after 1800 wore the stovepipe shako; this had been generally introduced at the turn of the century. The brass plate in front as worn by the artillery had the Royal Cipher in the centre within a Garter. All this was set on a trophy of arms and below was a mortar between pyramids of cannon-balls. The coat was now made with short tails and closed down the front. The yellow braid on the buttonholes had 'bastion' ends. Both long blue pantaloons with short gaiters as well as white breeches with longer gaiters were worn at this period. One shoulder-belt held the bayonet while the other had the pouch with the powder-horn attached by means of a red cord. A large oval buckle was worn at this date, the other ranks' belt-plate not appearing until later. The powdered hair was still worn with a large queue, usually false. A few years later the queue was officially abolished, much to the soldiers' pleasure. The large ruffle worn in the late eighteenth century had now dwindled to a small portion of white at the opening of the collar.

About 1812 the stovepipe shako gave way to one with a false front and plaited cords, also known as the 'Belgic Cap'. The white plume was now worn on the left side, with a waterproof cover as was the shako itself. This was a necessary precaution as in wet weather the rain-sodden shako soon went out of shape. The jacket remained in the same style.

Overalls were now normally worn on service, and these were white in the Peninsular War but blue-grey at Waterloo and on other occasions. The carrying of a musket was a considerable encumbrance to an artilleryman serving a gun, so this was subsequently discontinued and instead of a bayonet the second belt carried a brass-hilted sword. Artillerymen at Waterloo when overrun by the French cavalry had occasion to defend themselves with these heavy weapons.

The light cavalry had developed a leather helmet with a fur crest, sometimes known as the 'Tarleton' helmet. As civilian gentlemen had taken up a version of the felt 'bowler' hat, the headdress was a combination of these two. The fur crest gave a superficial likeness to the leather helmet as did the gold cords, but the lightness of the felt hat produced an article easy to wear and yet capable of warding off sword cuts.

The coat for overseas service had the lapels capable of buttoning, at least for a portion, in the centre of the chest. Its two gold epaulettes indicated the rank of an officer. The crimson sash round the waist was by 1792 slim and elegant, not the earlier pattern which went round three times, and the straight cut-and-thrust sword was suitable for gentlemanly duels but not of much value against firearms. Topped boots were needed for a mounted officer and also for a dismounted one who had to combat the mud of Flanders.

3
CONTINENTAL ARMIES

The Austrian and Hungarian Army

The Austro-Hungarian Empire dated from only 1804. Before then, the Emperor Francis I had been Emperor Francis II of the Holy Roman Empire, not of Austro-Hungary. Whereas France and Britain were homogeneous states and Spain had a form of traditional unity, the Austro-Hungarian Empire had none. It embraced Germans, Hungarians, Czechs, Slovaks, Croats, Ukranians, Poles, Russians, Romanians, Italians, and Belgians with no bond except that of a common emperor.

Family loyalties began the Prussian involvement against France in alliance with Leopold of Austria, who was brother to Marie Antoinette; the French replied in April 1792, attempting to isolate the Austrians by attacking Belgium.

A Prussian force, under the Duke of Brunswick, moved into Lorraine and captured the fortresses of Longwy and Verdun and, in July, the Austrians entered France from the Netherlands and besieged Lille. But in September the Prussians were repulsed at Valmy in the Argonne by untrained and undisciplined revolutionary levies which had, however, the support of the royalist artillery; the Prussians withdrew into Germany, and the French followed up, occupying Mainz, Worms, and Frankfurt. The French commander, Dumouriez, relieved Lille and, invading the Netherlands, defeated the Austrians at Jemappes. Brussels fell and the whole province was overrun. Another French army, attacking Piedmont and the kingdom of Sardinia, took Savoy and Nice.

In the First Coalition formed that August there were no fewer than fifteen member states. These, however, were disunited and split by jealousies and there was bad feeling between Austria and Prussia over the second partition of Poland.

Both Prussia and Austria had underestimated the effect of the French national revival on the morale of the revolutionary forces and both were distracted by a common fear of the Russians to the rear. Austria was involved with the Turks. But in 1793 the Austrians in the Netherlands attacked Dumouriez, who had meanwhile advanced into Holland, defeating him at Neerwinden. Dumouriez then deserted the revolutionary cause and went over to the enemy. A British force under the Duke of York, joining up with the Austrians in the Low Countries, invaded France and invested Dunkirk. The Spanish entered southwest France and British sailors occupied Toulon.

Defeat, however, only made the revolutionaries redouble their efforts and brought the fanatical

A heated, turbulent conference of Austrian generals.

The miner officer of the Austrian army wears a cornflower blue or dunkelhechtgrau *tunic with cherry red facings. The plume he wears is that of the engineers, wholly black rather than the black and yellow of sapper and miner officers.* (Ottenfeld/Osprey)

Austrian soldier of Pioneers wearing the summer field service uniform of 1809. In this year the Pioneers exchanged their tunics for the general service frock-coats (Rock) worn by other engineers. He also wears the new headdress. (Ottenfeld/Osprey)

A sapper officer of the Austrian army in 1800 wearing his summer field service dress, with the black and yellow plume, blue tunic with cherry red facings and lining, and straw-coloured trousers. (Ottenfeld/Osprey)

The picture shows an Austrian officer of artillery and a 'kanonier' before the turn of the nineteenth century. The kanonier carries the leather case, and wears a long pigtail. The high tops to the boots were very practical as knee-pads.

extremists to the fore. General conscription for military service was introduced for the first time and nearly half a million men were called to the colours. This was a departure from the methods by which professional armies had been raised up to this time and was to revolutionize warfare for the next century and a half.

In a series of offensives from the autumn of 1793 onwards the revolutionaries drove the Spanish and British out of France and overran the Austrian Netherlands once more. The Duke of York was defeated at Hondschoote and the Austrians at Wattignies and Fleurus. Moving into Holland, the French then captured the Dutch fleet which was imprisoned in the ice. Holland capitulated and was virtually incorporated into France as the Batavian Republic.

In 1795, by the third partition between Russia, Prussia, and Austria, Poland had disappeared from the map of Europe. Austria already held Galicia (from 1772) and now shared with Prussia the ethnically Polish territories. Kurland, Lithuania, Volhynia, and Podolia had gone to Russia. Prussia, more interested in spoils to the east than in fighting what it regarded as Austria's and Britain's war in western Europe, made peace with France by the Treaty of Basle, agreeing, at virtually no cost to itself, that France should remain in occupation of the west bank of the Rhine; the loss of the small Prussian territories on the river was to be compensated by the gift of other lands, the property of German princes. Of the First Coalition, only Britain, Austria, and Piedmont remained in the war.

Britain, by virtue of its command of the seas, was unassailable, and by default France's main adversary became Austria. Austrian Belgium, rich in coal and localized industries, had already fallen to France. Milan was an Austrian duchy outside the Holy Roman Empire, and Tuscany and Naples both had Habsburg connexions; the Papacy was unpopular in Paris and a French ambassador had been murdered in Rome. Italy was rich and ripe for revolution against the Austrians, the Papacy, and the Spanish Bourbons, and France had a liberating message to give the world. By this reasoning, not all of it illusory, the Italian campaign was decided upon.

The brilliantly successful campaign in Italy conducted by Napoleon against the determined but outfought Austrians culminated in the armistice signed at Leoben, with the French no more than fifty miles from Vienna.

By the Treaty of Campo Formio, signed in October 1797 between Napoleon and the Austrians, the Habsburgs ceded to France the Belgian Netherlands and recognized the left bank of the Rhine as being France's eastern frontier. In addition, northern Italy went to France as a French-controlled Cisalpine Republic. The Republic of Venice, an independent state occupied by the French without just cause, was made over to Austria by Napoleon to recompense for her losses. Britain was the only enemy of France remaining in the war.

Defeat of the French in Egypt by Britain gave nations on the Continent new hope against Napoleon. The destruction of the French fleet at Aboukir Bay by Nelson was the decisive factor in bringing about the Second Coalition composed of Britain, Turkey, Russia, and Austria.

Two types of Austrian helmet and cuirass showing development from 1805 (left) to 1827 (right), by which time ornamentation has been greatly reduced.

Austrian impetuosity and Russian incompatibility were responsible for both nations being soundly defeated by the French. Tsar Paul withdrew his forces from the war; Austria needed defeats at Marengo and Hohenlinden to be persuaded to make terms at Lunéville in 1801. All the same, when, after the peace of Amiens in 1802, a Third Coalition was decided on, Austria again rushed headlong into campaigning for Italy.

Once more the bulk of the reinforcing formations was allocated to that theatre. Archduke Charles, the only Austrian general who had consistently beaten the French (but not Bonaparte), was the Commander-in-Chief there. The Archduke John had a further 25,000 men in the Tyrol. In consequence there were too few troops left for what was to be the main theatre of operations in Bavaria, where Mack commanded a force of about 80,000 men. Mack's army met an inglorious end, for in September of 1805, having begun to advance westwards across the River Inn towards Ulm, it drew upon itself several French armies which, by their rapidity of manoeuvre, contrived to encircle an Austrian force of 49,000. Only one division, under Schwarzenberg, escaped and made its way safely to Bohemia. The remainder, faced with great odds, were obliged, on 20 October, to lay down their arms.

Archduke Charles was ordered north with 80,000 men of the Army of Italy, but he arrived too late to save even Vienna from enemy occupation. He withdrew to Hungary.

Meanwhile, a Russian army under Kutuzov had been marching westwards in order to make a junction with the encircled Mack, and got as far as the River Inn. On the approach of the victorious French forces, Kutuzov retreated back into Bohemia and Moravia, where he was joined by the Austrian division which had escaped encirclement. A further Russian army and more Austrian formations joined at Olmutz, bringing Kutuzov's strength up to 90,000 men.

In answer to Napoleon's demand for immediate surrender, the Emperor Francis procrastinated. The young Tsar Alexander had been to Berlin trying to imbue a little spirit into Frederick William, the King of Prussia, and when the two emperors met at Olmutz, Alexander brought the good news of a Prussian ultimatum to Napoleon, and the promise of Russian and Prussian military aid. Francis thereupon determined on striking a further blow against the French.

Bonaparte had arrived at Brünn in Moravia with an army of 100,000 men and, knowing that the Archduke Charles was near, he determined to bring the cautious Russians to battle. So he extended his 100,000 men over a frontage of ninety miles as if in an

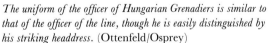

The uniform of the officer of Hungarian Grenadiers is similar to that of the officer of the line, though he is easily distinguished by his striking headdress. (Ottenfeld/Osprey)

The private of the Hungarian Infantry, seen here in his summer field service uniform, wears light blue trousers where his German counterpart would wear white, with black cloth gaiters. (Ottenfeld/Osprey)

observation line, his dispersal being such as to invite attack. The Allied force clumsily ambled forward a little. Napoleon conformed by retiring, as if to encourage his enemy; at the same time he thinned out the French right, leaving open the route to Vienna. Meanwhile, in anticipation of what he believed to be Kutuzov's attack, he rapidly concentrated over 70,000 Frenchmen behind the Goldbach stream. Then, as soon as the Russians had come down from the Pratzen plateau, he hurled his main force against the weakened Russo-Austrian centre.

The battle of Austerlitz began at 7.30 a.m. on a wintry December morning and lasted until 5.00 p.m. It was Napoleon's boast that out of thirty or more

The grenadier of the German Infantry of 1809 is easily recognized by his tall cap, bordered with fur, with a metal badge-plate in the middle and a cockade to the right. (Ottenfeld/Osprey)

The major-general here wears the normal uniform for German Infantry officers, his rank being distinguished by the zigzag gold stripe that can be just seen on the cuff. (Ottenfeld/Osprey)

battles, Austerlitz was the easiest and most decisive of his career. Russian troops, temperamentally unsuited to fighting alongside allies, being by nature suspicious and obstinate to the point of arrogance, ran away, cursing the Austrians as they did so. Both Alexander and Francis had to flee for their lives. For the Allied loss of 26,000 men and eighty guns, the French suffered only 7,000 casualties.

Miners and sappers of the Austrian army at work. Because most of their work was undertaken close to enemy lines they wore the protective helmet and cuirass; this pattern is of c. 1812.

An officer (in bicorn hat) and other rank (in shako) from the Austrian transport (Fuhrwesen) corps. The corps was responsible not only for wagon movement but also for all artillery horse-teams.

Austerlitz forced Austria out of the war and caused the King of Prussia to make terms very rapidly, though a brave second ultimatum issued by him prompted the French to invade. He was defeated at Jena and Auerstadt despite a considerable numerical superiority during the latter battle; it was not until Blücher reorganized the once magnificent army of Frederick the Great that it was able to make its mark.

The end of the Holy Roman Empire's dominance by the Habsburgs gave the Emperor time to rebuild his shattered nation.

The Austrians used the peace from 1806 to 1809 to good advantage by reorganizing their army. The Archduke Charles was given the mammoth task of making a united force from the various bodies of the Austro-Hungarians. The steadiest and staunchest arm was its German infantry and this took the brunt of most of the fighting. The Bohemian and Moravian elements tended to be politically unreliable and more prone to desertion, particularly since the Austrian was often viewed as a foreign ruler and oppressor. The Hungarian was in yet a different category, for he regarded himself as superior to the Austrian in war: but though he was usually a better horseman, he lacked the qualities of steadiness and stamina that make a good infantryman. Hungary did play a full part against the French but lacked the enthusiasm that had been evident under Maria Theresa.

The many minorities proved hard to accommodate in the army, particularly the Croats and the Romanians. Unlike the pandours and irregular hussars of the Silesian Wars, there was no place for the many *Frei Korps* in the Napoleonic era. The *Frei Korps* were eventually converted into regular light infantry but, since they were temperamentally unsuited to this employment, they were disbanded in 1801.

The Archduke Charles's reforms covered both the infantry and the cavalry and in particular the application of their tactics. But it was in the reorganization of the artillery that he was most concerned. Charles had learned much from the French and he determined to concentrate the control of the artillery at the highest possible level. The line guns, previously decentralized to infantry, disappeared in accordance with the French practice (although Bonaparte was in fact to restore them in 1809), and the Austrian artillery was built up as an independent supporting arm.

In 1808 the Austrian artillery took into use the Congreve rocket, from which was developed a two-barrelled 5-cm rocket. The launchers, which weighed only 19 lb each, fired a 6- or a 12-pounder shell, twenty-four launchers comprising a battery. For siege work 16- and 28-pounders were also used. Rockets were originally manned by the *Feuerwerkscorps*.

The 1805 Treaty of Pressburg, which had lost Hungary Dalmatia and cost Austria the Tyrol (ceded to Bavaria), was not to be forgotten and it left behind a passion for revenge. Although the Archduke Charles was to lose the next battle against Napoleon, his work in reorganizing the army, and in particular the artillery, had a marked effect on Austrian fortunes in the next five years. For Austria had not ceased to rearm since Austerlitz.

In April 1809 the Austrian Emperor, Francis, with a recently-found confidence in the new efficiency of his armies, and without seeking allies, as the German champion declared war on France.

The declaration was not unexpected, for Austria's feverish rearmament could have had no other aim. Napoleon advanced from the Rhine at the head of a large army and by his rapidity of movement outmanoeuvred Archduke Charles. Vienna was abandoned. Two engagements at Aspern and Essling came as an unpleasant surprise to the French, and Napoleon fell back to the island of Lobau.

Charles had at his disposal about 200,000 men, of whom 36,000 were horse and 23,000 light infantry *Jäger*, and 760 guns. His newly-reformed forces were organized on the French model and subsisted on the French requisition system. A further 200,000 *Landwehr* were in reserve, although these were indifferently trained and equipped and had only a reinforcement value. As against this, however, Charles had been obliged to detach 47,000 to the Archduke John in north Italy and leave a further 35,000 behind under the Archduke Ferdinand in Galicia to protect the rear from possible intervention from Poniatowski's troops in the Grand Duchy of Poland.

Meanwhile, Bonaparte remained inactive on the Danube to await the arrival of the reinforcements from Italy which raised his strength to 180,000 men. Then, emerging from Lobau, he fell on Archduke Charles's Austrian force which he outnumbered by nearly three to two. On 5 July the French won the Battle of Wagram, about ten miles north of Vienna. But it was a hard-won decision and the Austrians had proved a formidable foe; and, though they lost 36,000 men, Archduke Charles marched off the field with over 80,000 men in good order. There was no pursuit and no rout.

Austria made peace in October; it had to pay a large indemnity and reduce its army to 150,000 men, losing yet further territory – Salzburg, Illyria, and West Galicia (Little Poland). The new peace enabled Bonaparte to transfer 140,000 troops to Spain, bringing the total there under Masséna to over 300,000 men. The Spanish War was already becoming what Napoleon afterwards called 'France's ulcer'. After Wagram the French Emperor tried to consolidate his own position and that of his Empire by divorcing Josephine and taking a new wife, Marie-Louise, Archduchess of Austria and daughter of Francis I. When his son was born in 1811 Napoleon recreated for him the old Germanic title of the King of Rome, used by the early emperors.

The Uhlans, to whom this trooper belongs, had comparatively recently become regular troops of the Austrians, Russians, Prussians, and Poles. His peculiar headdress derives from Turkis and Polish origins. (Ottenfeld/Osprey)

The private soldier in the German Infantry of c. 1804 wears the traditional white summer field service uniform. This year saw the removal of pigtails in the German Army. (Ottenfeld/Osprey)

The German Jäger *non-commissioned-officer wears the basic line equipment that can be seen; facings and linings are in green and the tunic could be sky blue or* hechtgrau. (Ottenfeld/Osprey)

General service saddle of the pattern used by most German cavalry and horse artillery.

Francis had been valiantly supported by his Hungarian subjects, and 1809 marked the end of the old *insurrectio* militia when it came to battle for the last time at Gyor. Francis's courageous attempt to free Austria and Germany had failed because of the disunity and selfishness of the German princes and the timidity of the Prussian king.

Although Prussia took no part in the Franco-Austrian War of 1809, its army having been reduced at Napoleon's order to a ceiling of 42,000 men, the Austrian rearmament, and its effect, had not gone unnoticed in Berlin. Civil and military reforms were set in motion there by Stein and Hardenberg and by Scharnhorst and Gneisenau. Serfdom was abolished and the rigid class barriers removed; army officers were no longer appointed solely from the nobility and promotion was to be on merit, tempered by seniority. Arms, tactics, and methods were revised. But, most important of all, Scharnhorst hit on the obvious but no less ingenious scheme of the short-service engagement, which enabled Prussia to raise an additional and substantial reserve force, without exceeding the limits placed on the active part of the army. By this means Prussia was able to put into the field a force of nearly a quarter of a million men in 1814.

Economically Russia was the loser by the new anti-British alliance and the Continental blockade, since the main market for Russian goods was in Britain; the loss of customs revenues to the government contributed to the steady depreciation of the currency. At the end of 1810 St Petersburg, in a fit of pique against the French, replied by the imposition of a heavy tax on the importation by land of luxury goods, which in fact were mainly of French origin. Paris protested. In December of that year and January of 1811, Napoleon annexed to France the whole of the north German coast, including the Duchy of Oldenburg, which belonged by marriage to Alexander's sister, Catherine.

During 1811 the uneasy truce with Napoleon became more strained and Alexander looked about for allies. The Austrian royal house, linked recently by marriage with France, was for the moment uninterested. Prussia was too fearful. Russia did, however, improve its relations with Sweden. Meanwhile, Kutuzov, in command in the south, was ordered to come to terms with the Turks. By the Treaty of Bucharest, Alexander abandoned the Serbs to their fate and gave up his conquests of Wallachia and Moldavia, keeping only Bessarabia, the eastern portion of Moldavia between the Dniester and the Pruth. Alexander then looked to Britain for another alliance.

Alexander had made use of the remaining two years of peace to improve the efficiency of his armed forces. In 1810 his main military adviser Arakcheev left the War Ministry to undertake the reorganization of the artillery and the supply of all warlike equipment. His successor as War Minister was a Livonian, Barclay de Tolly.

The last approach to reason was made by the Tsar to the French Ambassador, General Lauriston, in April of that year. Alexander said that he was prepared to accept the indemnity offered by France to the Duke of Oldenburg and would modify the Russian customs system which discriminated against French imports. On the other hand, he insisted on freedom to trade with neutrals as he thought fit and, fearful for his own security, demanded that French troops should evacuate Swedish Pomerania and Prussia. He went so far as to say that if there was any reinforcement of the French garrisons on the Vistula he would consider this an act of war.

Napoleon made no reply to these demands but kept up diplomatic activity merely to gain time, for he had already decided to invade Russia. In May the French

Emperor arrived in Dresden preparatory to taking over the field command. Alexander was already at Vilna with his armies.

Against the Russian covering forces of about 225,000, Napoleon's *Grande Armée* numbered over 500,000, but of this total only a half were Frenchmen. The remainder of his force were Germans, Poles, Italians, Spaniards, Portuguese, and Croats, many of them doubtful and unwilling allies.

The Austrian contingent with the *Grande Armée* totalled only 30,000 troops and these were handed over grudgingly. When Bonaparte asked that the Archduke Charles should be made available to command them, the Prince bluntly refused to have anything to do with the business. The command then passed to Karl Philipp, Prinz zu Schwarzenberg, an officer of cavalry who had seen service against the Turks during the war of 1788 and 1789, becoming a major-general in 1796 and *Leutnant-feldmarschall* in 1800; his last military duty had been the command of a cavalry corps at Wagram. Thereafter he had been employed on diplomatic missions and had been the Austrian Ambassador in Paris: it was presumably because of this that Napoleon had asked for him. According to Austrian sources, he was instructed by Metternich to endeavour to keep his force intact and to give the French the least possible assistance.

Since the Austrian element of the *Grande Armée* was so small a detailed description of the 1812 campaign in Russia would be out of place here. Napoleon entered Russia in June, but Barclay de Tolly declined to come to grips with the invader and merely gave ground. Bonaparte's progress was dilatory because he waited in vain for Alexander to come to terms. De Tolly was replaced by the aged Kutuzov who finally gave battle at Borodino. Moscow was abandoned and fired. Bonaparte stayed too long there before deciding to retrace his steps, and when he began his return march the winter was already upon him. Kutuzov's army was still in being and the terrible Russian winter destroyed the *Grande Armée*. Very few of that half million returned. Kutuzov, true to hs his nature, was disinclined to pursue the French beyond the Russian borders. Alexander, however, insisted that Russian forces should enter Germany, for the Tsar had come to look upon himself as the saviour or Europe.

In December 1812 Yorck's Prussian troops, without authority from the King of Prussia, went over from Macdonald's French corps to the Russians.

Prussia welcomed the entry of Russian troops as liberators from the French yoke. The timid monarch, Frederick William, was forced to follow and, in the following March, declared war on France. Kutuzov took command of a Russo-Prussian army, until his death in April, when he was succeeded by Wittgenstein. Only western Germany and the Rhineland remained to Napoleon.

By April, however, Napoleon had taken to the field again and, at the beginning of May, von Lutzen drove the Russians and Prussians back beyond the Elbe. Three weeks later he defeated them again at Bautzen, but this time the Russians yielded the field in good order and were shortly ready for battle once more. Wittgenstein lost his command to Barclay de Tolly.

Austria meanwhile used its good offices to attempt to arrive at a peace settlement. Napoleon was willing to talk, since every day gained strengthened his position. By August it was apparent that Bonaparte was disinclined for peace, except on his own terms, and war was resumed, Austria joining Russia and Prussia.

Napoleon won the two-day battle of Dresden, but a few days later Barclay won a victory at Kulm.

The Austrian Field-Marshal Schwarzenberg, in spite of, or perhaps because of, his diplomatic missions, had always been an enemy of Bonaparte and he had been one of the strongest advocates for war against France when he had returned from Russia. In 1813 he was appointed Commander-in-Chief of the Austrian Army of Bohemia.

The Allies, Austrians, Russians, and Swedes, with a total force of about 320,000 men were moving into Saxony. Napoleon had only 190,000, but he was operating on interior lines and he intended to defeat his armies singly before they should unite. Bonaparte's first intention had been to advance on Blücher's Prussians and Bernadotte's Swedes who lay somewhere to the north of Leipzig, but he turned off south-eastwards in order first to meet Schwarzenberg's Austrians who were moving towards Leipzig from the east. Schwarzenberg was in fact lying between the Pleisse and Elster Rivers in a disadvantageous and exposed position, but Napoleon did not care to attack until Macdonald should arrive. Marmont, too, had been delayed.

Meanwhile, Blücher, who was over seventy years of age and had commenced his military career as an

The rear view of the Austrian army soldier of Miners (1809) shows how he carried his heavy entrenching spade and pistol. The sabre can also be seen under the spade. (Ottenfeld/Osprey)

Although drivers in the Austrian Transport Corps had been allowed since 1772 to wear brown as did the Artillery, they still usually wore white tunic and breeches. Facings, however, were yellow. (Ottenfeld/Osprey)

officer of Swedish cavalry, had decided that he could wait no longer for the completion of the concentration of the Swedish Army. Bidding Bernadotte, who had formerly been one of Napoleon's generals, follow him when he was ready, he and his Prussians set off alone for Leipzig. *En route* they came across

Marmont's force, also on the move, and a fierce battle developed about Möckern between Frenchman and Prussian. Bertrand's forces had already become involved in another engagement near the bridge at Lindenau, and it soon became obvious that Marmont would not reach Napoleon on that day of 16 October 1813.

That morning Schwarzenberg had given battle to Napoleon, attacking the heights of Wachau. At two o'clock in the afternoon Napoleon ordered Murat's 10,000 cavalry to attack Schwarzenberg's centre: this it did successfully and captured twenty-six guns. On the French side the battle then hung fire since Napoleon had quitted the field to see what was happening at distant Möckern, and Schwarzenberg's counter-attack forced Murat back and regained much of the lost ground.

During the next day there was a lull in the fighting and this enabled further Allied reinforcements to arrive and deploy, Austrians under Hieronymus von Colloredo, Swedes under the Frenchman, Bernadotte, and Russians under the Hanoverian, Bennigsen. These brought the Allied strength up to 300,000.

Napoleon should have attacked on 17 October or have withdrawn; for when the Allied offensive was resumed on 18 October he had little chance of holding his ground. After several hours' cannonade the massed columns of the Allies started their advance during the afternoon, and by late that night the French were in full retreat, throwing out a 30,000-strong rearguard. So ended the Leipzig 'Battle of the Nations'. The total Allied loss was 55,000; that of the French was unknown but was estimated between 40,000 and 60,000. They left 352 guns on the field.

This brought Napoleon's military and political career to an end temporarily; the hundred days which culminated in Waterloo put a final end to his ambitions. For Austria and Russia, the Battle of the Nations finished their direct involvement in the Napoleonic Wars; the Prussians under Blücher played their most distinguished part in the victory at Waterloo.

Uniforms

The pattern of the uniform worn by Hungarian and German infantry was similar in most respects except that German line soldiers wore white trousers and black buttoned-up cloth gaiters which came right up to the knee. Hungarian infantry almost invariably wore the pale blue trousers, close fitting at the knee and calf, usually with light blue facings on the frock-coated tunic. The general service shako was similar for officers and other ranks except that officers wore broad (and non-commissioned officers thin) gold stripes round the top brim of the cap. In addition, officers had a larger cockade and a thin gold metal border round the peak. Officers could be further distinguished from their men by black leather Wellington boots, worn almost to the knee, a thin gold braid stripe on the trousers, and a *porte-épée* concealed by a gold silk cummerbund sash. With the exception of the shako, the non-commissioned officers' uniform was the same as that of private soldiers except that the sabre continued to be worn, although it had been removed from most rank and file, the bayonet henceforth being carried in a sheath attached to the bandolier. The field-pack (*Tornister*) was by this time carried high on the shoulders supported by two shoulder-straps, a departure from the earlier equipment which carried it at the small of the back on a single strap over the right shoulder. The pack was surmounted by a cylindrical waterproof valise. A black leather ammunition-pouch was worn on the right side.

For the German infantryman, who wore the traditional white, with black gaiters and straw-coloured facings and linings, the pigtail (*Zopf*) disappeared in 1804 and the 1798 new-pattern headdress (*Kasket*) remained in general service until 1808. The greatcoat was dark grey. His accoutrements were bayonet-scabbard, water-bottle, haversack, pack, and cylindrical waterproof valise. The black leather ammunition *cartouchière* was worn on the right-hand side.

The *Jäger* was entirely distinctive and separate from the German light infantry, which was born from an amalgamation in 1798 of the many *Frei Korps* units of foot into fifteen battalions of the so-called light infantry. In 1801 they were all disbanded. The *Jäger* was the skirmisher and scout who formed part of advance and rearguards and manned the outpost line. He was in no way an irregular. The distinguishing feature of the *Jäger* was his green collar, cuffs, and linings. His uniform could be sky blue or *hechtgrau*, and the trousers were sometimes light green. Shoulder-straps were black with black and green tassels hanging forward on the left shoulder. He was equipped with a rifle, a long sword-bayonet, and a powder-horn. Otherwise the *Jäger* equipment is similar to that of infantry of the line.

By 1809 the former *Kasket* had recently been replaced by the black *Corséhut* with the left brim turned up and the cockade to the front. The uniform colouring was *hechtgrau* with the usual green facings and linings. The *Jäger* officer's uniform was similar

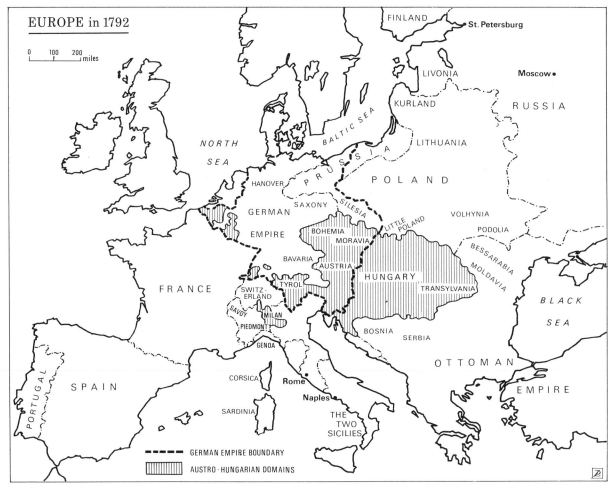

EUROPE in 1792

0 100 200 miles

FINLAND
St. Petersburg
LIVONIA
Moscow
KURLAND
RUSSIA
NORTH SEA
BALTIC SEA
LITHUANIA
HANOVER
P R U S S I A
P O L A N D
SAXONY
SILESIA
VOLHYNIA
GERMAN
BOHEMIA
LITTLE POLAND
PODOLIA
EMPIRE
MORAVIA
BESSARABIA
BAVARIA
AUSTRIA
HUNGARY
MOLDAVIA
FRANCE
SWITZ-
ERLAND
TYROL
TRANSYLVANIA
BLACK SEA
SAVOY
MILAN
PIEDMONT
BOSNIA
SERBIA
GENOA
OTTOMAN
CORSICA
Rome
EMPIRE
PORTUGAL
SPAIN
Naples
SARDINIA
THE TWO SICILIES

- - - - GERMAN EMPIRE BOUNDARY
|||||| AUSTRO-HUNGARIAN DOMAINS

Map of Europe in 1792 showing the boundary of the German Empire and the domains of Austro-Hungary.

except that he was expected to wear the *Schiffhut*, but in fact he often appeared in the *Corséhut* with a plume (*Federbusch*), either erect or hanging, fixed on to a gold *Jagdhorn*, with a gold clasp (*Agraffe*) on the turned-up brim of the hat. The officers' coats were supposed to be *dunkelhechtgrau*, but many retained the sky blue pattern, wearing gold epaulettes (which were forbidden to *Jäger* officers) with black tassels and a green fringe. Officers wore gold buttons, gold *Achselschnure*, a simple yellow metal guard to the sabre, with a green and gold sword-knot. When officers wore the light green trousers they usually sported a dark green double stripe. Officers' waistcoats were white, fastened with hooks, their black neckerchief stand-up collars being colloquially known as 'parricide' (*Vatermörder*). Officers' greatcoats were grey with black cuff facings and black collars.

The uniform of the officer of grenadiers had much in common with that of the officer of the line except for the distinctive headdress. The main differences between the uniform of the officer and the grenadier was that the latter wore neither gold sash nor *porte-épée*, had no gold border to the peak of his shako, had ankle-boots instead of knee-boots, and the piping on his trousers was gold and black instead of gold. He had light blue shoulder-straps (the officer having none) and his cuff device, as with infantry of the line, was in white wool instead of gold. And he wore the private's infantry-pattern short Hungarian sabre.

Until 1751 general officers had freedom to choose their own uniform and they wore what they pleased, and it was left to Maria Theresa to introduce a white half-length coat with rank designation shown by a broad golden ribbon stripe on the front facings and

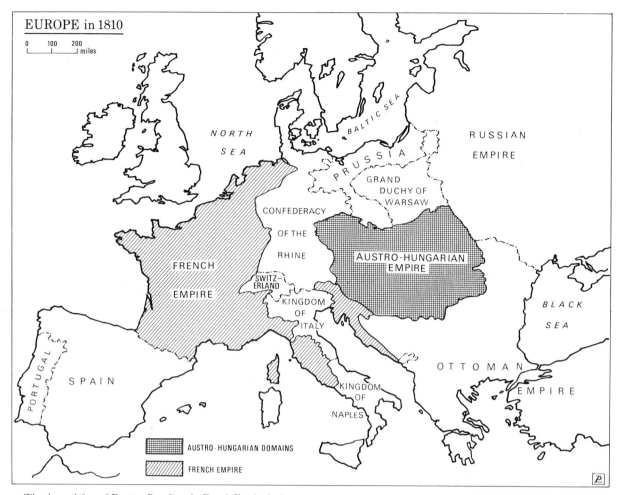

EUROPE in 1810

0   100   200
└──┴──┴──┘ miles

NORTH SEA

BALTIC SEA

PRUSSIA

RUSSIAN EMPIRE

GRAND DUCHY OF WARSAW

CONFEDERACY OF THE RHINE

SWITZ–ERLAND

FRENCH EMPIRE

AUSTRO-HUNGARIAN EMPIRE

KINGDOM OF ITALY

BLACK SEA

PORTUGAL

SPAIN

OTTOMAN EMPIRE

KINGDOM OF NAPLES

▦ AUSTRO-HUNGARIAN DOMAINS

▨ FRENCH EMPIRE

The changed face of Europe. By 1810 the French Empire had stretched well down into Italy and the south of Hungary. Poland has completely disappeared, and the Confederacy of the Rhine replaces the German Empire.

side pocket-flaps of the coat. This uniform remained virtually unaltered until the 'eighties when the gold rank-bars were altered to a zig-zag pattern, and gold buttons bearing an embossed star and an ornamented edge were introduced. In 1798 regulations for the first time made some distinction between field service (*campagne*) and parade (*gala*) uniforms. Greatcoats were henceforth to be *hechtgrau*, the same colour as worn by the 49th Regiment Vesque (later Hess), field-marshals wearing red-and-gold-embroidered collars and cuffs. The general officer's gold-bordered black headdress with the ten-inch-high green plume was to be worn only for parades. General-adjutants had the traditional green coat originally worn firstly

by the horse-grenadiers and then by the Emperor Joseph's *Chevaux-légers des Kaisers* (afterwards *Uhlan Regiment 16*). By an Imperial command of 1765 this coat was conferred on all general-adjutants; it had the red linings and facings of the original-pattern coat but with the addition of general officers' buttons. The general-adjutant wore a plain black headdress with a general's green plume; his waistcoat was straw-coloured, with his rank shown by the broad gold border stripes; the woollen breeches were of the same colour. Infantry field officers' boots and a gold-mounted sword completed his uniform. *Flügeladjutanten* (ADCs – usually to the monarch) wore the same dress as *General-adjutanten* except that they had white buttons instead of gold, and a sabre instead of a sword.

The major-general wore the dress for German general officers, his rank being shown by the zigzag

Austrian mounted Jäger *(on left), wearing* lichthechtgrau *with grass green facings and linings, and a Light Dragoon wearing the dark green coat inherited from the former horse-grenadier. The horse furnishings and shabracks are the same for both.*

These pictures show the horse artillery of the Austrian army in action. The gun's crew is carried on the 'sausage seat' in front of the barrel of the gun.

gold stripe on the cuff. Hungarian cavalry general officers wore an entirely different dress, somewhat similar to that of a hussar, with a half-worn *Pelz*, a *Kolpak* with a plume of heron's feathers, a red dolman, red trousers or overalls with a gold seam stripe, gold spurs, a red *sabretache* with the imperial arms in gold, and a sabre with a bright steel scabbard.

In 1798 all dragoon regiments and the *chevaux-légers* regiments (which were themselves the successors of the horse-grenadiers and carabiniers of Maria Theresa's reign) were amalgamated to form light

dragoons. They retained the dark green coat of the former horse-grenadier. The collar and cuff facing for 1 and 4 Regiments of Light Dragoons were scarlet, for 2 and 14 gold, 3 and 5 orange, 6 and 8 pink, 7 sulphur yellow, 9 and 15 black, 10 and 12 sky blue, and 11 and 13 Pompadour red. Where two regiments wore the same coloured facings, one wore yellow buttons and the other white.

The horse-furnishings and shabracks for both the mounted *Jäger* and the light dragoons were identical. In 1801, however, the light dragoons were split once more to form dragoons and *chevaux-légers*.

The hussar, who originated in Hungary as a border fighter, continued to be the mainstay of the German

117

An Austrian artillery 'kononier' with a 6-pounder gun. An ammunition-container is incorporated in the design of the carriage and trail and is covered by a seat on which rode the gun detachment.

and Hungarian light horse, for he could be used as line cavalry and yet apply himself to a dozen specialist tasks, in particular, scouting and reconnaissance, outposts and picquets, escorting and convoying, and deep raiding. He never carried a lance but was armed with a carbine, a pair of pistols and a light-pattern sabre with the single *Bügel* guard. At the turn of the century there had been little change in the traditional dress of the hussar except that he had taken the buttoned-up overall trousers into use, these being worn over the boot. The shako, used by infantry and other arms, had also been adopted either additional to, or instead of, the fur cap and coloured bag. The circumference of the shako was greater at the top than at the lower hatband so that it presented a funnel-like effect; officers and non-commissioned

officers wore the customary gold-edged peak and gold stripes round the top of the cylinder. All hussars continued to wear the dolman, sabretache, and leather ammunition pouch. The hussar horse-furniture comprised the regulation leather saddle set on a horse-blanket, with a pair of pistol-holsters, cloak or greatcoat strapped across the pommel, and the water-bottle and spare blanket attached to the cantle. The whole was covered by the coloured shabrack and a lamb's-wool pelt, being secured by a leather surcingle strapped over pelt, shabrack, saddle, and girth. The carbine shoulder-strap fitted with a metal swivel, continued in use.

The *Uhlan* came to Europe by way of Turkey, for the word comes from the Turkish *oghlan*, meaning a child, and began its military use in exactly the same way as the Italian *infanterie*. From the border-fighting Turkish light cavalry, the use of the word and of the troops passed into the Polish Army, as the distinctive pattern of the headdress shows, and from there, in the middle of the eighteenth century, it spread to Saxony and Austria. In the Silesian Wars the uhlan was often a mounted irregular as the hussar was before him. Eventually the uhlan became part of the regular forces (in the Russian, Prussian, Polish and Austrian service) and he was in fact a light cavalry lancer.

The duties of engineer (*Ingénieur*) and sapper officers overlapped, yet both were separate and distinct departments within the same corps, officers and other ranks being maintained on their own lists and establishments. They took command over each other according to rank and seniority, but a sapper officer could not transfer to the engineers without taking a special examination or having served as an instructor in the Engineers Academy. Sapper and miner officers could, admittedly, be posted to fill engineer vacancies, but this could be done only as a temporary measure and when engineer officers were not available. Before 1800 it had been customary to recruit other ranks by transfer from the infantry, and in consequence the sappers received the unfit or the unwanted; but from 1801 onwards new regulations demanded that new recruits, direct from civilian life, should be young and strong bachelors, at least five feet four inches in height, and be able to read and write German fluently.

Engineer, sapper, and miner officers wore a very similar uniform, a cornflower blue or *dunkelhechtgrau* tunic with cherry-red facings and linings, and straw-coloured trousers and waistcoats, the buttons being of yellowsmooth pattern. Greatcoats were of the same colour as the tunics. All other equipment was of infantry pattern. Miner and sapper officers wore the ten-inch high black and yellow plume, whereas engineer officers wore a black one. The other ranks of both miners and sappers wore the *Corséhut*, similar to that of officers except that it was without the gold rank-band and had no leather edge, buttons, or chin-strap. The rank and file of both sappers and miners were dressed in *hechtgrau* throughout, with cherry-red facings (*Egalisierung*), artillery-pattern boots or twill gaiters, and carried a musket or a pistol in a black leather holster and an artillery sabre. The sapper sword was of a distinctive pattern in that it was saw-toothed for a length of fifteen inches on the back edge of the two-foot blade and had a modified haft and guard so that it could be used as a saw. The *Obermineur* and *Obersappeur* wore *porte-épée*, gloves, a hazelwood cane, and a woollen border to the hat.

A Prussian hussar officer's equipment and shako, sabretache, and cartouchière.

In 1801 the companies of miners consisted of four officers, two *Feldwebel,* two *Minenmeister,* two *Minen-führer* (the sapper equivalent ranks were *Sappeurmeister* and *Sappeurführer*), and *Ober-, Alt-* and *Jungmineur.* In addition to their specialist duties they were used on a wide variety of labour tasks.

The pioneers and the pontoniers had both been raised later than the other three engineer corps, and until 1809 the pioneers were under the direction of the general staff (*Generalquartiermeister*) and not the Director-General of Engineers, and because of this had green and not cherry-red facings to their uniforms. The pioneers performed many of the tasks done by sappers and their employment covered the construction of earthworks, fortifications, roads, storm assaults, demolition, bridging, obstacles, flotation, construction of accommodation and field-ovens, and so forth, and they owed it to Radetzky, who had once served in a pioneer troop, that they maintained an existence almost in opposition to the sappers. Another reason, too, which enabled the pioneers to remain in being, was that it was a Czecho-Slovak preserve, fifty per cent of all recruits being Bohemian, thirty-five per cent Moravian, and only fifteen per cent German, its ranks being almost entirely tradesmen or specialists, carpenters, masons, millers, ditchers, and gravediggers. The pontoniers had a strength of six companies, but were not on the same technical plane as the pioneers on whom they relied for assistance in bridge-building; their only training was in elementary watermanship.

As elsewhere there was a bitter controversy within the Austro-Hungarian Army at this time as to whether artillery should be fought centralized at the highest possible level under an artillery commander, or decentralized, all or in part, under the control of the infantry. The Archduke Charles believed that infantry should be self-sufficient and self-reliant and, when he became *Generalissimus* in 1809, the line guns disappeared and artillery became an independent supporting arm. Artillery was reorganized into field batteries (eight 3-pounders or 6-pounders), siege-batteries (four 6- or 12-pounders or four 7- or 18-pounder howitzers) and horse-batteries (six-pounders). About four batteries usually made up a company and sixteen to eighteen *kanonier* companies made a regiment, although the total number of companies of all types could exceed this since it often included a *Feuerwerkscompagnie* for rockets, companies of bombardiers who manned the howitzers and mortars, and a *Handlanger* battalion. The *Handlanger* soldier was not a gunner or bombardier, since he merely acted as labour on the gun-sites and helped to protect the guns, yet in emergency he could often act as gun-crew. Austrian artillery was an élite corps and enjoyed many privileges, and from 1810 onwards, by an imperial benefice, it was given higher pay and pensions than the rest of the army.

Artillery dress was the roedeer-coloured short tunic for summer wear and a half-length mounted-pattern coat for winter, with the traditional artillery *ponceau-rot* facings (sky-blue for the *Handlanger*). The head-dress was worn with or without the gold and black plume, rank being shown by the gold-bordered edge. A corporal commanded two field guns.

The Russian Army
On the death of Catherine the Great her son Paul became Tsar of Russia. Suspicion of all around him, well founded as it turned out, froze any military initiative against France and prevented a coherent foreign policy. He had become incensed at Napoleon's seizure of Malta, which made it possible for Great Britain to persuade the Russians to join the

This trooper is a mounted infantryman whose job is to manoeuvre rapidly and then fight on foot. However, he would sometimes be required to fight as a cavalryman and usually carried a short sword.

second coalition against the French. In 1799 Paul recalled the great general Suvorov from retirement to fight in Italy with the Austrians as allies. But a defeat of another Russian army in Switzerland under

NCO of the Tversky Dragoons; note the straight sword of the heavy dragoon.

A student officer of a fashionable cavalry regiment.

Korsakov infuriated the Tsar, who considered the Austrians were to blame. He quarrelled with Britain over their occupation of Malta, returning to the policy of Catherine by signing with Denmark and Sweden a treaty of armed neutrality directed against Britain. By 1801 it was hard to tell who Paul's friends or enemies were. Theoretically he was at war with France and he had broken off diplomatic relations with Austria. But he was ready to fight his ally England, and had sent 20,000 Cossacks eastward to invade India.

In March 1801, in a palace *coup* in which Pahlen, the Governor-General of St Petersburg, and a small group of army officers together with the Semenovsky Guards took part, Paul was murdered. He was deposed, it is believed, with the foreknowledge of his son and successor, Alexander.

The new Tsar, like his two brothers Constantine and Nicholas, was fascinated by the parade-ground, to the exclusion of other forms of training for troops. Like his father in his conduct of foreign policy, he could not decide whom to trust, and so made terms with Britain and France, though the relationship with both was uneasy. He made overtures to Prussia who

had not been at war since 1795. But it was Napoleon, who had intended all along to fight the Russians, who pushed Alexander into open hostility by crossing Russian territory on his way to attack Austria. Alexander, deciding to help the Austrians after their defeat at Ulm in October 1805, took on the French at Austerlitz. This was Alexander's lesson that war was not to be learned on the parade-ground and that he himself was without ability as a field commander. After the battle he wept, blaming Kutuzov for not insisting more strongly on avoiding battle.

Russian troops were not temperamentally suited to fighting alongside allies. An earlier Anglo-Russian expeditionary force in the Low Countries had been a failure. A second Anglo-Russian expedition made up of 5,000 British and 13,000 Russians, together with a Neapolitan army of 40,000, had more fortune in 1805 in that they cleared the French from Italy.

By this time Austria was out of the war and Alexander's attention reverted once more to Prussia, with whom he concluded a secret agreement. On 26 September 1806 the King of Prussia sent an ultimatum to Napoleon demanding that French troops quit German territory east of the Rhine. Napoleon's

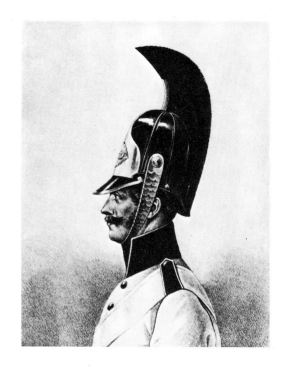

Samples of cavalry headdress as worn on ceremonial occasions. The wearers are Cuirassier NCOs. These wildly impractical helmets were sometimes worn in battle.

reply was to march troops which inflicted two successive defeats on the Prussian Army at Jena and Auerstädt. On 25 October Napoleon entered Berlin and French troops occupied Prussian Poland as far east as Warsaw. Russia was now directly vulnerable to the French Army which had arrived at its frontier.

An indecisive battle at Preussich-Eylau followed, the Russians losing 26,000 dead. A new war against Turkey and a decisive defeat by the French at Friedland forced Alexander to make peace with France, declaring war against Sweden instead. The years of peace were uneasy but gave Alexander time for badly-needed military reforms. There was some change in the field grouping, in accordance with the Napoleonic pattern, the tactical formation now being the division.

The infantry of the field army was, by 1812, made up of 170 regiments of 511 battalions, there being three battalions to the regiment. On mobilization, however, this number of active field battalions was due to be reduced to 401, since the second battalion in each regiment was to find reinforcements to bring the first and third battalions to full strength and throw off

an élite company, these companies being grouped into new grenadier battalions. The remnant of the second battalion became the depot battalion for the mobilized regiment of two field battalions. A guard battalion at war strength numbered 764 men, and one of the line 732.

The 170 first-line infantry regiments were formed into twenty-eight divisions (six regiments to the division of which two were light infantry). Of these twenty-eight divisions, eighteen were deployed in the west, four in Moldavia, three in Finland, two in the Caucasus, and one on the Black Sea.

In addition to the 286,000 first-line infantry of the field force there 103 garrison infantry battalions and 216 infantry battalions of the reserve, in all another 230,000 men, organized into eighteen reserve divisions, numbered from 30 to 47 inclusive. These divisions had a command and administrative, rather than a tactical, function; for the battalions were drafted into the field army after the war started, and the reserve divisions eventually disbanded.

In 1811 there were seventy regiments of regular cavalry, totalling 440 squadrons, of which eighty-one squadrons formed the depot squadrons in time of war. The remaining 359 field formation squadrons numbered 49,000 horse. These troops, including the guard and Ukrainian Cossacks, were regular cavalry. The

Emperor could easily raise, however, a further 100,000 cavalry from the Cossack hosts, at least eighty-two regiments from the Don, ten from the Black Sea, fifteen from the Ukraine, and more elsewhere. It was to these so-called 'cavalry irregulars', particularly to the Cossacks of the Don, that Kutuzov owed much of his success during the French retreat in 1812 and 1813.

There were twelve regular cavalry regiments in Moldavia, two in Finland, and three in the Caucasus. The remaining fifty-three were in the west.

The artillery totalled 159 batteries/companies of which thirty-two were depot companies. Each company of foot artillery was 250 men strong and was equipped with twelve guns. Horse artillery batteries usually varied by designation. Heavy batteries had four 20-pounders and eight 12-pounders, while light batteries had four 12-pounders and eight 6-pounders. Divisional artillery brigades normally had one heavy and one light company.

The engineer corps comprised twenty-four companies of pioneers and the same number of pontoon companies which, by 1812, had been taken over from the artillery.

The Russian Army in 1812 numbered 700,000 men in all, not including the Cossack hosts or the *opolchenie*, the home guard militia.

In the early summer of 1812 the troops in western Russia were deployed in three armies. The first, under Barclay de Tolly (who still retained his post as Minister of War), of six infantry corps and four of cavalry, was made up of 127,000 men and 500 guns. The second, under Bagration, of two infantry corps and two of cavalry, had only 45,000 men and 200 guns, while the third, under Tormazov, of three small corps and a corps of cavalry, totalled 46,000 men and 160 guns.

The uneasy peace was broken in 1812 by Napoleon, who had already decided to invade Russia. On 24 June 1812, without formal declaration of war, the *Grande Armée* crossed the Niemen on its way into Russia.

Fortunately for the course of the Napoleonic Wars the Russians did not risk all on one engagement. They fell back slowly westwards. Constant harassment of the stragglers by the Russians had already reduced the French army to 200,000 by the time it reached Smolensk in mid August. The War Minister Barclay de Tolly decided to give battle there, but sensibly wanted a line of retreat. Since Barclay was insistent that he should first secure his withdrawal route to Moscow before accepting battle, he dispatched Bagration's 2 Army to Dorogobuzh, about eight miles further east. Raevsky's 7 Corps inside Smolensk was relieved by Dokhturov's 6 Corps.

On the afternoon of 17 August Napoleon directed Ney, Davout, and Poniatowsky against the defences in front of the suburbs and before evening had reached the city walls. By nightfall much of Smolensk was on fire and Russian losses had been heavy – estimated at 20,000. Barclay de Tolly gave the order for the retreat to be resumed and by daybreak the Russian columns were already several miles to the east. The next day on the Valutina plateau, due east of Smolensk, Barclay was attacked again by Ney. If Junot had co-operated in the outflanking movement, Barclay would have lost a large part of his remaining 100,000 men.

The delay at Smolensk and the time wasted waiting to see if the Russians were willing to surrender

On the left a non-commissioned-officer and on the right two privates of the Eger regiment. The one on the right is in parade uniform.

Grenadier headdress at the time of the Napoleonic Wars lacked nothing in ostentatious style. On the left the NCO has a white plume and varied accoutrements but the grenadiers on the right are also very formally attired.

meant that the summer was now nearly finished. Not until 24 August, very late in the Russian campaigning season, did Napoleon decide at last to make for Moscow.

Kutuzov had received some 30,000 reinforcements, many from the *opolchenie* of very indifferent quality, and he decided to give battle near Borodino on the main highway to Moscow. The French forces had dwindled to about 125,000 and by now were slightly outnumbered by the Russians. After a preliminary engagement on 5 September, the main battle began two days later and lasted throughout daylight. The French were left in possession of the field but their losses amounted to 30,000. Before the end of the day, General Rapp, already wounded, commented to the Emperor that he 'would be forced to send in the guard'. To which Napoleon replied that he would 'take good care not to', as he did not want it destroyed. By not committing the guard Napoleon may have permitted Kutuzov to escape. But in the event, the decision was of relatively little importance,

for Napoleon himself sealed the fate of the *Grande Armée* by remaining too long in Moscow. The weather did the rest.

On 13 September Kutuzov held the celebrated council of war at Fili and decided to give up Moscow rather than destroy his army. He left the old capital, moving off south-eastwards on the Ryazan road; French troops entered the city the next day. The day after the occupation fires destroyed much of Moscow; there was little of the reward there that they had expected.

On 18 October the Russians surprised some French under Murat and inflicted 4,000 casualties. That day Bonaparte gave the order to evacuate Moscow and begin the march for home.

When the spearhead of the *Grande Armée* left Moscow it was 100,000 strong. Except for that of the guard, discipline had already been eroded by the loss of good leaders and, more particularly, by the demoralizing effect of looting and excesses. Caravans of plunder were included in the withdrawing columns. Very soon there was a shortage of food which could be met only by slaughtering draught animals. The heavy autumn rains turned the roads into a morass, in which animals foundered and artillery and carts had to be abandoned.

Two grenadiers from the Tavrichesky Grenadier Regiment. Note the very long overcoat – usable as a blanket – and the considerably less utilitarian and over-ornate headgear.

The Cossacks, with the advantage of great mobility, and now heavily reinforced, were endlessly troublesome and it was dangerous to leave the highway in search of shelter or food. Scores of partisan bands raided and butchered isolated detachments. Terrible atrocities took place. Yet the French themselves were by no means guiltless, Russian soldier prisoners being done to death in their thousands when they could no longer be fed or guarded.

At the beginning of November, Napoleon reached Smolensk, where Victor's reserve army held the reinforcements and stores. The withdrawing columns had already been reduced to 40,000 men. Even so the stores were not sufficient, for the undisciplined mass of soldiery plundered the depots, emptying the base in a few days. The bitter cold sapped the French strength, and in the further battles about Krasny Napoleon suffered more serious losses. When the *Grande Armée* fell back on the Berezina it was scarcely 20,000 strong.

The uniform of the junior officer is now much more practical than in former years; in this winter parade uniform he could fight if required. (Youens/Osprey)

Meanwhile, on the far northern flank, Wittgenstein's corps attacked Macdonald near Polotsk, drove him back to the south-west, and took the French military base at Vitebsk. In the south Admiral Chichagov had marched from Moravia and, joining up with Tormazov, moved northwards, seizing the great French supply base at Minsk. Chichagov then attempted to cut off the withdrawal route of Napoleon's centre column by occupying the crossing-places on the Berezina at Borisov. From the third week of November onwards the Russian Army began seriously to dispute French movement, Wittgenstein and Chichagov doing their utmost to destroy the remnants of those troops who had withdrawn from Moscow. But Kutuzov, impervious to the anger of General Sir Robert Wilson (who was serving with the British Military Commission in Russia), displayed his customary inertia in failing to come to the support of his countrymen, excusing himself on the grounds that Napoleon's forces were still formidable and that it was foolish to risk defeat when cold and hunger would finish off the Frenchmen anyway.

In the event, this is what happened. The weather suddenly became colder. Wittgenstein and Chichagov, unsupported by Kutuzov, were unable to drive in Victor's rearguards, but cold and panic destroyed most of Napoleon's forces and camp-followers waiting to cross the Berezina. Napoleon left for Paris.

Including those troops who had deserted in the course of the advance, about 400,000 of the original half-million-strong *Grande Armée* failed to return from Russia. Russian losses were probably in the region of a quarter of a million. In October all three allies converged on Leipzig for the 'Battle of the Nations', on which field, between 16 and 18 October, Napoleon was decisively defeated.

On 30 March 1814 Alexander entered Paris. Napoleon abdicated on 11 April and was exiled to Elba. The Russians played no further part in the war.

In 1812 before the recommencement of the war the 170 regiments of field infantry were made up of six guard regiments; fourteen grenadier regiments; ninety-six fusilier regiments; fifty light infantry regiments (not necessarily rifle-armed *eger*); four marine regiments.

The first-line infantry numbered in all 286,000 men.

The seventy Russian cavalry regiments comprised six guard regiments: Gentlemen of the Guard; Horse Guards; Hussars; Dragoons; Lancers; and Cossacks (all the guard regiments had five squadrons except for the Cossacks which had three); and sixty-four cavalry of the line regiments; eight cuirassier regiments; thirty-six dragoon regiments; eleven hussar regiments; five lancer regiments; and four Ukrainian

Cossack regiments. (Line regiments had five squadrons except for the hussars and lancers which had ten and Ukrainian Cossacks which had eight.)

In 1790 the Russian Army was organized in the following way:

56 REGIMENTS OF CAVALRY

Horse Guards	1
Horse Grenadiers	1
Horse-Eger	2
Dragoons	14
Cuirassiers	5
Carabineers	13
Hussars	14
Cossacks	6

104 BATTALIONS OF INFANTRY

Guard Regiments	3
Grenadier Regiments	13
Fusilier Regiments	56
Eger Corps	10
Corps Battalions	22

DEPLOYMENT OF RUSSIAN TROOPS IN MAY 1812
1 ARMY (BARCLAY DE TOLLY)

CORPS	Infantry Bn.	Cavalry Sqns.	Cossack Regts.
Infantry			
1 Wittgenstein	28	16	3
2 Baggovut	24	8	
3 Tuchkov	24	4	1
4 Shuvalov	23	8	
5 Constantine	27	20	
6 Dokhturov	24	8	
Cavalry			
1 Uvarov		20	
2 Korf		24	
3 Pahlen		24	
Platov			14
	150	132	18

Cavalry helmets had to be strong enough to stop or turn a blow by a sabre, but soon acquired fanciful ornament according to the whim of the commander.

2 ARMY (BAGRATION)

CORPS	Infantry Bns.	Cavalry Sqns.	Cossack Regts.
Infantry			
7 Raevsky	24	8	
8 Borosdin	22	20	
Cavalry			
4 Sievers		24	
Ilovaisky			9
	46	52	9

3 ARMY (TORMAZOV)

CORPS	Infantry Bns.	Cavalry Sqns.	Cossack Regts.
Infantry			
Kamensky	12	8	
Markov	24	8	
Sakken (depot corps)	12	24	
Cavalry			
Lambert		36	9
	48	76	9

Uniforms

The design of the uniform of the Kievsky Grenadier Regiment shows the type that was in general use around 1800; it is derived from that of the Gatchina

Infantry. For the fusilier, the tunic (known as the *caftan* or *mundir*) was in the dark green colour traditional to the Imperial forces, and the pattern was not very different from that worn by the infantry of the Empress Catherine II. There were variations by regiments; some wore white metal buttons and different-coloured facings; some Moskovsky regiments wore the parallel cuff woollen braid vertically instead of horizontally; but in the main the general appearance for the line-infantry tunic was not greatly different. Underneath the tunic the soldier wore a red neckerchief, a shirt or waistcoat of the same colour as the pantaloons, usually white but in some regiments citron or straw-coloured, and in cold weather a sheepskin half-jacket or *shuba*. Pantaloons were of wool in winter and linen in summer, and the spats or leggings were of strong, black, canvas-like cloth. All the leather equipment for the soldier's accoutrements was of Russian *yuft* except for the pack which was of black calf leather. The crossed white shoulder-straps were traditional in the Russian Army for nearly 150 years. The cap was of a very old-fashioned pattern long discarded in western Europe, with a thin metal covering bearing a crown, the inscription 'God is with us', and a large Imperial eagle. The musket was of Prussian design, having a walnut butt and stock, brass and steel fittings with bayonet cleaning-rod and ramrod attached. In length it was one *arshin* fourteen *vershkov* (about fifty-two inches) or, with bayonet

This fusilier of the Kievsky Grenadier Regiment is wearing winter field service uniform of a pattern which was in general use at the time. His tunic is of traditional green. He carries a sword as well as a bayonet and might need both, for his musket was unreliable. (Youens/Osprey)

This dark green uniform of the corporal in the 24th Eger regiment is rather unusual, for most Eger regiments wore light green. As this is a walking-out dress he is not carrying his carbine and bayonet. (Youens/Osprey)

This trooper of the Guards Cavalry corps is wearing everyday uniform. As a light cavalryman he carries a straight sword, a pair of pistols, and a carbine. (Youens/Osprey)

fixed, sixty-eight inches. It was inaccurate and had an effective range of less than 200 yards. The soldier carried a sword as well as a bayonet and a grey unlined winter greatcoat.

By a new army regulation of 7 November 1807 all heavy infantry, that is to say line and grenadiers, were to have distinguishing patches on the greatcoat collar and on the tunic collar and cuffs, denoting the seniority of each regiment in the division: red for the first, white for the second, yellow for the third, dark green with thin red piping for the fourth, and sky blue for the fifth.

In addition, grenadier regiments were to wear a distinctive colour on the shoulder-straps (*pogoni*): yellow for St Petersburg, white for Siberia, and red for the remainder, the number of the division, where applicable, being shown on the grenadier's shoulder-strap, in gold for officers and stitched for other ranks. The new pattern of uniform showed French Napoleonic and Prussian influences and was to remain in service, little altered, for the next forty years. The greatcoat, carried rolled over the shoulder in traditional fashion, was grey, the winter woollen pantaloons being exchanged in summer for Flemish linen. At his back the grenadier carried a sword and bayonet-scabbard, a black leather *lyadunka* or cartridge-case bearing the same regimental crest (the flaming grenades) as was worn on the cap, a black calf leather pack and a waterbottle. The regulation load for the pack was two spare shirts, one pair pantaloons, footwrappings (instead of socks), a soft forage cap, spare boots, drawers, twelve flints for the flintlock, three brushes, two graters, a button-stick, pipeclay and boot polish, and a housewife. The summer weight of the pack was 25 lb, in winter $26\frac{1}{2}$ lb.

Light infantry of foot (*eger*, from German Jäger) usually wore a light green uniform, but the colour of the collar and sleeve varied according to the number of the regiment. *Eger* never wore the coloured shoulder-straps (*pogoni*) as did the infantry and the other arms. The greatcoat was of regulation grey, without shoulder-straps, and in summer all ranks wore white trousers of unbleached linen. Some regiments wore coloured piping on the green pantaloons. As light infantry their parade and skirmishing order was without pack and other impedimenta, no sword being carried other than a sword-bayonet similar to that in use elsewhere a century later. The firearm was a short-barrelled flintlock with an eight-groove rifled bore, the bayonet mounting being on the right-hand side of the barrel. This rifle was first manufactured as early as 1775. *Eger* rifle battalions provided the skirmishers and screens, relying on their fleetness of foot and long-range fire, to cover the main body of infantry and artillery.

There was some variation in the uniforms of the foot *eger* regiments. Most were in light green uniforms, but they could also be found in dark green tunics and dark green or summer white linen overalls. The collar and cuff colours were of course another distinguishing feature, which varied between regiments. All *eger* regiments were, however, armed with the rifled carbine and all wore black leather belts and accoutrements. Unlike the line, other ranks never carried the sword but relied on the bayonet as the side-arm. The newly introduced stovepipe headdress was common in other armies of western Europe. For fatigue wear or in undress the stovepipe headdress was replaced by the forage cap with a drooping crown and hanging tassel, looking very much like the nineteenth-century nightcap.

The commanders of all formations of the size of brigade and above were part of the *generalitet*, another military collective borrowed from Prussia, although in the guard regimental commanders might be major-generals. Generals were usually classified, again German fashion, according to arm so that as full generals they were known as Generals of Infantry or Artillery. The pattern of the collar and sleeve braid was usually common to arms, however, except that the *General-Adjutant*, a designation bestowed also on admirals (who shared the army ranking system), had its own very distinctive gold braid pattern.

The guards cavalry was re-formed in April 1799 into a composite guards cavalry corps under the auspices of the Grand Master of the Order of St John of Jerusalem, and the Cross of St John was incorporated into the intricate cap-badge. The corps was designed to fill the very pressing need for light cavalry and the trooper was armed with the 1797-pattern broadsword, a pair of pistols carried on each side in the pommel holsters of pig leather (and known for this reason as *chushki* or pigs), and a carbine carried on the right-hand side and suspended by a swivel to the broad shoulder-belt of Russian red *yuft* leather running over the trooper's left shoulder. The shoulder carried the sabretache (*lyadunka*) commonly worn at that time by sword-carrying infantry as well as cavalry: the sabretache, like the *porte-épée* and scabbard, being in red moroccan leather, trimmed at the edges with raspberry-coloured silk and carrying on it a brass and silver star with the Order of the Cross. The horse is ridden, as with all guards cavalry, on the curb rein of the rather fierce long-cheeked Pelham bit, the lower chain being an ornament and not the curb chain which fits, of course, closely under the horse's chin. The uniform insignia is of particular interest, since its introduction commemorated the assumption by the Tsar Paul I of the Grand Mastership of the Maltese Order of St John.

The Sumsky Hussars claimed that they were one of the oldest regiments, if not the oldest, in the Imperial Army, having been founded, according to tradition, in 1651 as the town Cossacks of the frontier town of Sumy, near the Russo-Ukrainian border, about half-way between Kiev and Kharkov. These town Cossacks were in fact regular forces and had no connexion with the main Cossack hosts; during their long life the Sumsky cavalry had been Cossacks, dragoons, uhlans, and hussars. But even among hussars they were regarded as an aristocratic and exclusive regiment and the regiment was often included in the guard cavalry corps. In winter a blue-grey cloak with fawn fur edging was worn, together with heavier brick-red breeches with a white stripe at the edge. The long flowing shabrack saddle-blanket was blue-grey with white toothed edging, and bore the monarch's monogram at the rear.

Uhlans were light cavalrymen, armed with lance, sword, and carbine, first used by the Turks and then by the Poles in the Austrian service. Uhlans were adopted by Austrian, Pole, German, and Russian. The honorary Colonel of the regiment, the Tsarevich Konstantin, son of the Tsar Paul and brother of Alexander I, had taken up his residence in Warsaw where he was a great admirer of Polish troops and Polish women. The trooper wore the soft forage cap of the period. The dress for ceremonial parades was similar except that the forage cap was replaced by the tall square uhlan shako, with glazed peak and high plume, and the blue overalls by dark grey pantaloons buttoned at the side from hip to ankle. The usual two broad white leather shoulder-belts were worn, one on each shoulder and crossing at the chest, one for the sword and the other for the carbine.

Tartar cavalry often served as part of Cossack formations although they were, of course, in no way Cossack, and the Tartar uniform dress was a curious mixture of patterns. The Tartar trooper wore a uhlan shako, but his shoulder-belt, sabretache, and *porte-épée*, all of Russian red *yuft*, together with the sabre were of hussar pattern, except that they were without the usual white silk or wool edge trimming. This particular Tartar regiment was sometimes paired with a Lithuanian horse regiment which was similarly accoutred. The nine-foot lance was carried by a shoulder-sling when mounted, or held in the crook of the right arm when on dismounted guard duty. The white sling on the left shoulder was attached by a swivel to a carbine behind the soldier's back.

About 1812 there was much change in the detail of the uniform of the cavalry of the line, for the Kirnburnsky Dragoons could also be found with brass spurs, and a light green tunic, usually worn with the white cloth summer pantaloons. Each dragoon regiment was allotted a basic colour, although a single colour might be shared by several regiments, and this colour was common to the collar patch, the cuff, the shoulder-straps (*pogoni*), and the saddle-cloth.

By a St Petersburg order of 12 October 1811 the Astrakhansky Cuirassier Regiment and the Novgorodsky Cuirassier Regiment were ordered to change the colour of their uniforms, the Astrakhansky Regiment taking a plain yellow uniform while the Novgorodsky Cuirassiers took pink. Otherwise the design of their uniforms, in common with most other cuirassier regiments, was almost identical except for the collar and shoulder-strap colours.

Whereas the dragoon was meant to be the mounted heavy infantryman, the horse *eger* filled the need for mounted rifles. Like his cousin of the foot he was the skirmisher and the scout, finding the screens and standing patrols for cavalry as well as infantry. Yet he was supposed to be able to fight as cavalry, for he carried the heavy-pattern curved cavalry sword. His uniform was something between that of the horse artillery and the dismounted *eger*, and at his back he carried a black leather sabretache surmounted by the Imperial double-headed spreadeagle in brass. His horse shabrack was in dark green edged in red.

The engineer corps, including sappers, miners, and pontoon troops, were really an offshoot of the foot artillery and their uniforms had much in common. The grenadiers and artillery used the flaming

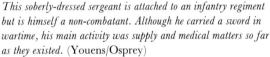

This soberly-dressed sergeant is attached to an infantry regiment but is himself a non-combatant. Although he carried a sword in wartime, his main activity was supply and medical matters so far as they existed. (Youens/Osprey)

Ryadovoi of Uhlans, Tsarevich Konstantin Pavlovich's regiment in undress uniform. He wears the soft forage cap of the period. (Youens/Osprey)

grenade or bomb as the regimental badge, and the engineer troops followed suit. The shako, except for slight differences in the badge and plume, was identical and the tunic was somewhat similar to that of foot artillery. The engineers, however, wore thick grey overalls in winter (white linen in summer) with the protective button-up gaiters. All other ranks of engineers carried the short sword as a side-arm.

The artillery had not long been accepted as an arm of the field army. Regarded hitherto as auxiliaries, the pattern of their uniform at this time showed the officer more like a country squire than a soldier. No epaulettes or badges were worn and there was little about the wearer, except for his straight and heavy cuirassier officer-pattern sword, to show that he was part of the Tsar's regular forces. Mounted, of course,

This officer of the Horse Artillery is wearing summer uniform. As the Artillery was a new addition to the service, the uniform has not yet acquired the distinctive detail of older regiments. (Youens/Osprey)

This Infantry general has several distinctive features. His sash has long tassels, and his epaulettes and collar are of distinctive pattern. His rank (whether major-general or above) is shown on his cuff. (Youens/Osprey)

he looked a little more imposing, usually on a bay charger with a dark green gilt-edged shabrack with the Emperor's monogram surmounted by a crown embroidered in gold in the corner and on the holster covers. The uniform of the horse artillery at the time was almost identical with that of foot artillery, but, by 1812, the horse artillery adopted a pattern of dress very like that of cuirassiers and dragoons with a high-

crested tall helmet, a short green tunic with a high black collar and cuffs edged in red, red and gold epaulettes, a white cummerbund, and grey trousers buttoned at the side from hip to ankle bone.

This corporal of the Sumsky Hussars is wearing the elaborate summer uniform of one of the oldest and most aristocratic regiments. Although Cossacks, they were regarded as a race apart from their less elegant though undoubtedly formidable compatriots. (Youens/Osprey)

This Unter-Ofitser *(corporal) of the Astrakhan Cuirassiers is wearing uniform of an unusual colour. The yellow colouring was adopted by the regiment as recently as 1811. The original cuirassiers took their name from the body armour on chest and back which was worn by earlier horsemen.* (Youens/Osprey)

A *bombardir* was later, like his British equivalent, a corporal of artillery, but at this time he was a private of artillery, a gunner, usually manning a mortar or howitzer. Except that he carried no musket, his equipment and his load were the same as that for an

infantryman. Across his shoulder he slung his greatcoat, and on his back he wore a black calf leather pack and waterbottle, a black *lyadunka* ammunition-case, and the *tesak*, a straight-bladed short sword. He appears to have carried no other weapons, for French reports described Russian gunners defending their guns against cavalry and infantry, using swords, rammers, and handspikes.

The horse artillery wore a distinctive headdress quite different from that of the foot and carried the mounted-pattern sabre. Ranks could be distinguished by the horsehair *sultan* or plume. A private soldier had a plume of white with black and orange at the root; a non-commissioned officer's was black and orange at the top and white below; a trumpeter's was red. An officer's was different again in design. Foreign spectators at about this time reported that the horse artillery also wore a uniform very similar to that of dragoons or cuirassiers, with the high fur-combed helmet, a green tunic and grey overalls buttoned up at the side.

The Russian engineers, sappers, and miners were, as we have said, an offshoot of the gunners and in 1805 the pontoon regiments were still listed under artillery. In consequence, the uniform was little different from that of the foot artillery, from which the *pontonier* could be distinguished only by his black shoulder-strap and the black cockade in the centre of the other ranks' shako. The *pontonier* could also be found wearing grey overalls, buttoned up at the side, instead of leather knee-boots. The wide white leather shoulder-belt carried a black leather ammunition-case displaying the Imperial double-headed spread-eagle in brass. The *pontonier* carried a curved half-sabre and not the foot-artilleryman's straight-edged *tesak*.

There were a number of small Greek colonies on the Black Sea ports, and Tsarist Russia gave refuge to fellow members of the Orthodox religion fleeing from the oppression of the Turk. Two Greek battalions had been formed, the first in the reign of Catherine II, really as an expression of Tsarist goodwill to the Greeks, and they were used mainly for guard duties. They were very colourful, but their arms and equipment were so obsolete that, when eventually they were committed to battle, they demanded modern Russian arms. But these, when received, were no improvement and caused the Greeks to mutiny.

The uniform had a green *caftan*, red waistcoat with gold sash, grey breeches, and black Hessian boots. Collar and cuffs were red; edging gold. The uniform of officers was similar, except that the gold edging was much wider and gold buttons were worn; private soldiers, on the other hand, had no gold braid at all. The difference between the first and second battalions lay in the variation of colours between waistcoats, shirts, cuffs, and collars, in green, dark green, and red.

Non-combatant officials formed a considerable part of the Tsarist Army and carried out a wide variety of functions. They manned the supply and transport service both inside and outside the regiments; they were the collectors of the wounded and were what passed in those days for medical orderlies, known as overseers (*nadzirateli*) of the wounded; they were the commissariat and the sutlers, the clerks, the draughtsmen, the artisans, and even the barbers; some were officials of officer grade, doctors, surgeons, auditors, paymasters, apothecaries, and priests. For the other ranks, the uniform was green with a red cap, and they wore the *tesak* sword and a cane for walking-out. Although they were classified as non-combatants, they carried a musket or pistol in time of war. Non-combatant officials of officer grade wore the everyday officer's green uniform, but their swords were of a distinctive pattern with a straight blade and a single guard on the hilt.

The Cossacks
The Cossacks served Russia well during its many wars, and no soldiers were more steadfast to the Tsar during the period of the Napoleonic Wars. The Don Cossacks, in particular excelled in his service. It was said, for example, that according to the official assessment they could raise only 19,000 troops in 1763. In 1802 this was raised to a maximum of 40,000. Yet, during the Napoleonic Wars, the Don Cossacks formed eighty-six regiments totalling over 50,000 men, of which 20,000 fell in battle or died on campaign. The other Cossack hosts provided a total of twenty-five regiments for field service against Napoleon.

Other so-called Cossack regiments were to be found serving the Tsar during this period. Yet they had no host and were hardly likely to be recognized as Cossacks by the men from the Don or the Terek. Many of these were in fact regular Tsarist cavalry, given Cossack names in deference to nationalist opinion. Nowhere was this more obvious than in the Tsarist Ukrainian Cossack regiments which appeared during the Napoleonic Wars. By 1816 the need had passed and the Ukrainian Cossack cavalry were

This Cossack Imperial Guard is in full dress with the standard
red tunic and baggy blue trousers. A plume and tassel are now
placed on the traditional cap. (Youens/Osprey)

This Ural Cossack is one of a squadron in the Imperial Guard.
His hat, although impressive, was so impractical that it was
withdrawn after a few years' service. He carries a pistol instead of
a carbine. (Youens/Osprey)

A Don Cossack. He wears an astrakhan cap and a caftan. Although he is a member of an élite Guard unit he has a poor mount. (Youens/Osprey)

converted into uhlans. In 1831 two further Ukrainian Cossack regiments came into being on the army lists, this time to deal with civil unrest in Poland, this possibly being a political manoeuvre to divert hostility from the Russian. These two regiments were eventually moved to the Terek where they became the Vladikavka Regiment. During the nineteenth century Ukrainian Cossack regiments alternately appeared and disappeared in the Tsarist ranks.

Many of the contemporary sketches and prints of Cossack cavalry during the early nineteenth century give the impression of well-mounted, uniformly equipped and superbly turned-out Tsarist lancers rather than Cossacks.

Cossacks rode their horses freely and with great agility and skill. From the Circassians they had learned the *djigitovka*, the circus showmanship and equestrian tricks. But horse-schooling or military dressage in the west European sense was largely unknown to them. Except in the Guards regiments, spurs were never worn in the nineteenth and twentieth centuries by Cossacks in the Tsarist forces, reliance being placed on a heavy whip (*nagaika*) which was part of every Cossack's military equipment. In consequence horses were rarely, if ever, ridden 'on the bit'. Nor did the Cossack horse, outside the guard, ever feel a curb, for the regulation bridle was a simple single-reined snaffle.

In addition to their own military structure the Cossacks had their own rank titles from the simple *kazak*, *prikazni* (corporal), *uryadnik* (sergeant), *vakhmistr* (common for all Russian cavalry sergeant-majors), *khorunji* (cornet), *sotnik* (lieutenant), *podesaul* (captain), *esaul* (major) and *starshina* (lieutenant-colonel). Thereafter they used Russian rank titles.

The Cossack's equipment consisted of a *papakha*, a busby usually of lamb's wool, a hood (*bashlik*), tunic, breeches, leather knee-boots, a forage cap and cover, an infantry-pattern greatcoat and a fur coat or pelisse. The Terek and Kuban Cossacks in addition wore the *cherkesska*, a long Circassian tunic with cartridge pockets sewn on either side of the breast, a *beshmet* or close-fitting Tartar waistcoat worn under the *cherkesska*, and a *burka* or black sleeveless felt coat. A proportion of the Don, Ural and Astrakhan Cossacks carried a cavalry-pattern lance without a pennon, for the front rank only, a Berdan rifle and a curved dragoon-type sword, except that the sword-guard was never fitted to the hilt. Unlike the cavalry of the line no bayonet was carried, nor a bayonet scabbard fitted to the sword-scabbard.

Uniform

Because the Cossack had to provide uniform and horse at his own expense, there was no accepted pattern or insistence on any uniformity of detail in his saddlery, his equipment or indeed in the colour or design of his uniform. Many Cossacks, officers as well as men, wore more or less what they pleased, and this appears to have been acceptable to the Tsarist military authorities. Some of the nineteenth-century plates depicting Cossacks were engraved in St Petersburg for Russian military magazines, and these tend to show the Cossack in a false light since he is usually portrayed as well-mounted, adequately accoutred, and superbly turned out. These artistic plates differ very much from the photographs taken at the end of the nineteenth century, where the peacetime squadrons of the Cossacks, even of the Imperial Guard, are revealed riding poor-quality, shaggy, and unkempt ponies with knotted bridlery, the troops themselves presenting, when judged by contemporary western standards, a wild, slovenly and unsoldierly appearance.

Even Viskovatov, the Russian authority on uniforms, is sometimes at a loss when called upon to describe Cossack equipment and dress, because of this lack of uniformity within regiments and squadrons. When describing the nineteenth-century uniform of the élite Don Cossack *Ataman* (the Tsarevich's) Guard Regiment, he says: 'All ranks were ordered to wear a belt, of no particular design or colour. But, in so far as it was possible, officers in a squadron and even in the regiment did try to wear one particular colour since it usually helped to establish identity. For the type of Cossack sabre in the Ataman Regiment there was no specially ordered pattern.'

There was, however, a general style of uniform and accoutrements which developed over the centuries. From the Zaporozhian Cossacks with their Tartar affectation and Turkish leanings, came the high conical fur hat with coloured crown or flowing bag together with the *caftan* coat, often with slit sleeves to permit freer use of the arm. These were perpetuated in the dress of the Don Cossacks and, for a time, in that of the Ukrainian Cossacks, the *caftan* becoming the long *chekmen* coat and the tall Turkish hat the *papakha*. In the earlier part of the nineteenth century

A typical Cossack feat of brilliant horsemanship and audacity. These activities date back to very early times and gave the Cossacks their colourful reputation. (Hulton)

(1803–60) there was a Tsarist attempt to Europeanize the Cossack dress and make it conform more closely to that of the Imperial cavalry of the line; in some respects this was achieved since the remaining Ukrainian and the Don Cossack regiments began to take on a rough Tsarist pattern.

The Ural and the Siberian Cossacks and their offspring, the Transbaikal, the Amur, the Ussuri Cossacks, and to a much lesser extent the Orenburg Cossacks, formed, however, another group. All except the Orenburg were much influenced by the recruitment of, and marriage with, the Siberian tribal peoples and in this respect they were less ready to conform to St Petersburg standards. The bitterness of the Siberian climate also had its effect, in that custom and clothing were developed according to need. Horses were never clipped. Coats were heavier; the great fur or sheep's-wool headdress looked like a bearskin rather than a Turkish fez. These Cossacks

have now disappeared from Russian military history.

Apart from these two main groups of Cossacks, the European and the Siberian, there remains the third family distinctive also in the pattern of its dress, the Caucasian, made up of the Terek and the Kuban Cossacks. Although the Terek Cossacks were the Great Russian descendants of an offshoot of the Don Cossacks, they have been in Caucasia now for over three centuries and have absorbed Caucasian tribal blood, customs, and dress, the cartridge-bedecked *cherkesska* and Circassian accoutrements and weapons. The Kuban Cossacks, although of Ukrainian stock and descendants of both Ukrainian and Zaporozhian Cossacks, have been in the Kuban for over a century and a half. These too have taken over Circassian dress and habits.

The dress and military uniforms of the Circassian and Caucasian Tsarist regiments, show a very marked similarity to those of the Cossacks, particularly to the uniform of the infantry and artillery of the Caucasian Line Cossack Hosts.

The Tobolsk Town Cossack belonged to a cavalry

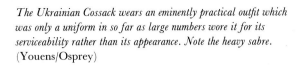

The Ukrainian Cossack wears an eminently practical outfit which was only a uniform in so far as large numbers wore it for its serviceability rather than its appearance. Note the heavy sabre. (Youens/Osprey)

The Zaporozhian Cossack has a distinctly Turkish and Tartar look. Note his pigtail, his moustache, and his turned-up shoes. His clothes are loose, baggy, and practical. (Youens/Osprey)

regiment based on the old Siberian Tartar capital of Sibir; the Tartar influence is shown in the buttonless *caftan*, sash, and baggy trousers and in the high lamb's-wool cap. This Cossack belonged to no host and may have come from an offshoot of the Siberian Cossacks, or, more likely, was a local recruit to a Tsarist-raised regiment based on the garrison town. For though the soldier received pay, uniform, and horse from the military authorities, yet he conformed to the Cossack pattern of the time in that he was a lancer, carrying an eight-foot lance with a toe- or stirrup-sling – but no shoulder-sling – and wearing a sword which was the forerunner of the common Cossack sabre, without a guard and with virtually no crosspiece, and was carried in its scabbard with the cutting edge to the rear.

The Ukrainian Cossack, like the Zaporozhian, wore exactly what he pleased but, although he may have fought as a member of the Zaporozhian Host for one or more seasons, he was influenced less directly by Tartar or Turk than by the Russian and the Pole. For this reason he tended to be much more Europeanized in his clothing and appearance, except that he commonly wore the long *caftan* and sash. The Zaporozhian Cossack wore Turkish or Tartar dress and used Turkish weapons, sometimes because he stripped Tartar dead and wounded and raided Turkish settlements, and sometimes because he was in the pay of the Ottoman Sultan on whom he relied for firearms. The only distinguishing feature about him, common to the whole Zaporozhian military order, was his shaven head, with a topknot which hung down the back like a pigtail. Although Tartars made up but few of their number, many Zaporozhians attempted to disguise themselves as Tartars or Turks. Others wore moustaches and beards. As has been said, the distinctive hat, the *caftan* (or the half *caftan*) and the slit sleeves became common to other Cossack hosts.

The mount of the Don Cossack of the Guard is small, cold-blooded and unkempt, and very undistinguished under its colourful saddle-cloth; it is ridden on a simple jointed snaffle and not on a curb, and, as the horse is normally ridden well forward of the bit, that is to say with its nose in the air, reliance is placed on a standing martingale to keep it under control and prevent it throwing its head. The bridle had only one buckle on the right-hand side (and one on the left under the cheek) and all other joins in the

This Tobolsk Cossack comes from the eastern regions and has the traditional lance and curved sabre. He wears a caftan held together by a sash and has a warm lamb's-wool cap. (Youens/Osprey)

An uglier side to the Cossack story. Here they are butchering French stragglers on the retreat from Moscow. The Russians were highly critical of French ruthlessness on the advance. (Hulton)

A charge by Don Cossack lancers. This is a stylized picture of a manoeuvre; in practice it would be considerably less controlled. (Hulton)

These Cossacks come from the Black Sea area and wear whatever is available and is convenient. However, their horsemanship was impressive even is their 'uniform' was not. (Hulton)

bridlery and harness are knotted for strength, there being no stitching or D-pieces. The saddle, on a regimental and very ornate shabrack, is fastened by straps and prevented from slipping by a breastplate formed by knotting the breast straps with the lower end of the martingale and the strap running under the horse's belly from the surcingle. The stirrups are of the normal heavy and wideiron or steel type common to western Europe; the horse was usually ridden in normal cavalry fashion with long leathers. The Cossack himself wore the tall black astrakhan cap, often with a chinstrap, and the short *caftan* now known as the *chekmen* with the slashed sleeve. The sword could be carried on the saddle or on the sword-belt; spurs were still worn – and continued in use in the Guard Cossack regiments throughout the nineteenth century. The carbine was carried in a peculiarly awkward position, attached by a clip and swivel from a shoulder-belt, so that it could be fired from the shoulder without first being detached.

The Ural Cossacks formed a squadron of the Imperial Guard. The Cossack's uniform of about 1800 appears to have already come under the St Petersburg influence particularly in the extravagant design of the hat; this was in keeping with the times, for helmets and shakos were being refashioned with high extensions. This particular type of hat appears to

This trumpeter in the Caucasian Guard Regiment has an impressive-looking horse but it was probably one kept for ceremonial occasions. Normally his mount would be smaller and less well-kept. (Hulton)

Count Platov, General of the Don Cossacks, set off to invade India in 1801. The expedition, a whim of the Tsar, was a failure. (Hulton)

have been withdrawn after only a few years in service. The loose baggy trousers were now worn outside the boots but the long *caftan* remained, secured by hooks and sash. The shoulder-sash with the swivel and catch, formerly for the carbine, was still in use, but a pistol had been substituted; presumably this was a handier weapon in close-quarter fighting and less awkward to carry in mounting and dismounting and at the trot and the gallop.

The full-dress uniform of the Cossack of the Imperial Guard in 1812 set the pattern for the uniform worn, with slight variations, by all the hosts, and the colours of red tunic and blue trousers were to be a distinguishing feature of the Cossack Guard's full dress throughout most of the nineteenth century. The *caftan* and *chekmen* had disappeared and the trousers taken on the very baggy appearance associated with the first two decades of the century. There was much else which was common to the military uniforms of

the European empires rather than to Cossackdom. The Cossack-type cap remained with its distinctive bag, but a plume and tassels had been added. Cavalry gauntlets and full white epaulettes appeared and the sword was of the heavy European cavalry pattern. As yet, however, there were no tunic facings and buttons. These were to come later in the century.

Blücher's Army

In the long struggle with Revolutionary France and with Napoleon, Prussia's share was less than pre-eminent. In successive coalitions she either had no part at all or played second fiddle to Austria, Great Britain, and Russia. But in the final campaigns from 1813 to 1815 she fell upon the French with all the fervour and energy of a modern *blitzkrieg*. This was due to Field-Marshal Prince Blücher, who led or drove his raw regiments to the fight with relentless vigour. The uncertainty displayed by the Prussian High Command in 1806 was not for him. His army of 1813–15, though it contained perhaps half the officer corps that had fought at Jena and Auerstädt, was nothing like the outdated machine that Karl Wilhelm Ferdinand, Duke of Brunswick had inherited from his uncle, Frederick the Great. The soldiers of the War of

The equipment of the Landwehr *Infantry of the Prussian Army was less defined than that of the line. The officer of the 1st Pomerainian Regiment seen here is wearing the* litewka *and trousers instead of breeches and gaiters.* (Roffe/Osprey)

This officer, of the 3rd Silesian Regiment in the Prussian Army, is wearing the litewka *in blue with yellow facings. His shabrack would also be blue with yellow trimmings; his main arm is a lance.* (Roffe/Osprey)

The private of the 1st Westphalian Regiment in the Prussian Landwehr *Infantry wears a blue litewka with dark green facings. His shako is of regular issue.* (Roffe/Osprey)

Liberation showed up poorly on the parade-ground, but they made up in enthusiasm for any lack of the old Prussian precision in matters of drill and turn-out.

In the campaigns of 1813 and 1814, at Dennewitz, on the Katzbach, and at Leipzig the Prussian Army recovered the self-respect which it had lost not so much on the battlefields of Jena and Auerstädt as in the shameful surrenders that followed. The Prussian Army of 1813 was very different, not only in appearance but in spirit, from that of 1806. It was the same as that of 1815; it was Blücher's Army.

In 1804 the King of Prussia had 9,752,731 subjects living in his domains, of whom 4,860,747 were men. The Canton system of recruiting permitted numerous exemptions; but even so, in 1805, there were 2,320,122 men liable to military service. By the Peace of Tilsit (9 July 1807) the population of Prussia was reduced to 4,938,000. The loss of rich provinces reduced her territory from 5,570 to 2,877 square miles. Of her fortresses only Graudenz, Pillau, Kolberg, Glatz, Silberburg, and Cosel had Prussian garrisons. The rest were garrisoned by the French. In less than a year, Prussia, from being the foremost among the German military powers, had become one of the least.

The mobilization of 1813 began on 9 February when the royal authorities in the temporary capital at Breslau declared conscription for the regular army. Earlier still, on 28 January 1813 an Armament Commission had been set up to supervise the mobilization and expansion of the army. Its members included Hardenberg, Scharnhorst, and Hake. It was on that date that Scharnhorst resumed his old post at the head of the War Department.

Royal orders for mobilization were issued on 12 January, 1 February, and 2 and 18 March 1813. The first, ironically enough, was in response to a French request for additional troops. It gave a pretext for bringing regiments up to establishment size and for calling up artillery, pioneers, and reservists.

By an instruction of 7 February it was laid down that subalterns who had served in 1806 and 1807 were eligible for immediate promotion, while any capable cadet, or suitable NCO could be commissioned forthwith.

On 3 February Hardenberg had announced the formation of Volunteer Jäger units, appealing to the propertied classes, who were exempted from conscription, to volunteer. This measure brought in

The drummer belongs to the 24th (4th Brandenburg) Regiment. Note how his greatcoat is rolled up and worn round the body, kept tidy by the piece of brown leather to the lower right of his chin; this was normal Prussian practice. (Roffe/Osprey)

young men of good family, who were officer material. In the first months of 1813, 2,798 volunteered and by the summer the total had reached 7,800, enough to provide a sizeable pool of young officers. At first the Jägers, who had to provide their own equipment, were given preferential treatment. But the strict discipline of the old Prussian Commands soon showed, and they soon had the penalty of whipping applied as freely to the volunteers as to any ordinary recruit.

By the time Prince Eugène de Beauharnais had withdrawn his French troops from Berlin on 4 March, the alliance with Russia had been signed (28 February). On 16 March King Frederick William felt confident enough to declare war on the French Empire. He appealed on the next day to the people of his country to support the now national struggle, and began the war with the following resources:

FIELD ARMY
1,776 officers; 66,963 men; 20,105 horses; 213 guns.
MEDICAL, TRAIN AND TECHNICAL TROOPS
2,643 men; 3,625 horses.
SECOND-LINE TROOPS
615 officers; 32,642 men; 650 horses; 56 guns.
GARRISON TROOPS
398 officers; 22,277 men; 1,743 horses; 148 train (*Knechte*).

The total amounted to 127,314, but half the men were recruits without much training. There was little artillery; muskets were hard to come by and there were not enough horses. Flints for muskets were so scarce that the Berlin porcelain factory was ordered to make *ersatz* ones.

On 21 April a *Landsturm* force was brought into being. It was to be a guerrilla army, armed with flails, rakes, pikes, and axes, and was to carry out a scorched-earth policy upon the approach of the enemy. It was not uniformed – indeed uniform for the *Landsturm* was expressly forbidden.

Students of uniform will observe that whereas most units of Blücher's Army wore Prussian blue, many of the shakos and cartridge-belts had a decidedly English appearance. But arms are even more important than uniforms and it is not too much to say that without English weapons the Prussian Army would have been on the same footing as the *Landsturm*. By the end of June 1813 British arms were arriving in the Baltic ports. By 15 July 40,000 muskets and 8½ million cartridges had been received. Cannon, powder, ball, wagons, and uniforms arrived in quantities. Altogether the Prussian Army was issued at least 113,000 English muskets in time for the autumn campaign of 1813. They were needed, for by June 1813 the Prussian Army numbered nearly 150,000 men. The *Landwehr*, recruiting vigorously, raised a total of 120,000 men by mid-July: Lithuania, East and West Prussia to the Vistula, 20,000 men; Prussia west of the

Vistula, 6,620; Silesia, 49,974; New Mark, 7,941; Electoral Mark Brandenburg, 20,560; Pomerania, 15,409.

In the 1815 campaign the Prussian Army was organized into Headquarters and four army corps. There were no divisions. Each corps had four infantry brigades, each about the same size as a French infantry division. Each corps had two or three brigades of cavalry and between six and eleven batteries of artillery as well as a company of pioneers.

The corps varied in strength:

	1	2	3	4
Infantry	29,135	27,002	22,275	27,459
Cavalry	2,175	4,471	1,981	3,321
Gunners	1,054	1,501	999	1,307
Guns	*88*	*80*	*48*	*88*
Pioneers	204	74	63	151
Total	32,568	33,048	25,318	32,238

Staff
The Headquarters Staff under von Grölmann numbered only six officers. The remainder of the Army Staff numbered forty-nine and included the officer commanding the artillery, the commandant of Headquarters, surveyors, surgeons, an auditor, the provost-marshal, and others. In all the Prussian Headquarters amounted to fifty-eight officers.

A corps staff comprised about twenty officers and a brigade staff about five.

The officers of the Army Headquarters included Leutnant-Colonel Count von Nostitz, Blücher's ADC who gallantly rescued his general at Ligny; Major von Winterfeldt, who was severely wounded when, while taking an important message to Wellington, he imprudently rode too near the French outposts; Captain von Wussow; and Captain von Scharnhorst.

At Leipzig Yorck's staff included Colonel Katseler, Major Count Brandenburg, and Major von Schack. In the same battle, Gneisenau's ADC was Captain Stosch.

Cavalry
In June 1808 the Prussian cavalry was 12,871 strong, including 535 officers and 1,766 NCOs. Since the whole army numbered only 50,047, this was a reasonable proportion of mounted troops, but, since 4,634 of the men were on more or less permanent leave, the regiments can scarcely have been in a very high state of efficiency. When in 1813 the Prussian

The cannoneer in the Silesian Brigade of the Prussian artillery wears a dark blue litewka *: his epaulette straps are of the Silesian colour, yellow, for this reason not matching the collar and cuffs.* (Roffe/Osprey)

The adjutant of cavalry seen here wears a uniform closely resembling the Austrian, though it is in fact Prussian. Collar, cuffs, and turnbacks of the litewka *are dark green, and there is a red stripe down the trouser leg.* (Roffe/Osprey)

Army was expanded to some 200,000, serious difficulties were encountered. Of these the worst was the lack of horses. It actually proved impossible to mount all the veteran cavalry troopers available. Farm and draught horses which no self-respecting cavalry officer would have looked at in 1806 were pressed into the service – but the French were in similar straits.

The Prussian cavalry held their own pretty well during the 1813–15 period, though their best units were not as good as the élite regiments of Napoleon's cavalry. Nor were they anything like as well mounted or equipped as the British and King's German Legion cavalry of the day.

In the Waterloo campaign Blücher's cavalry numbered only 11,948.

	Cavalry	Total
Napoleon	20,000–22,000	125,000
Wellington	14,000	c. 110,000
Blücher	11,948	123,172

This dragoon of the Prussian Army's 5th Brandenburg Regiment carries a sabre but is temporarily without his carbine. This regiment had sky blue cloth schabracks with black edging; it was normal for dragoons that schabracques should follow the colour of the tunics. (Roffe/Osprey)

The officer of the Prussian 1st Königin Dragoons is wearing the kollet *style of jacket in dark green with red facings, with brown trousers.* (Roffe/Osprey)

Moreover Blücher's cavalry was all allotted to his various corps. Unlike Napoleon he had no true reserve cavalry. The proportion of cavalry in each corps varied considerably.

Corps	Squadrons	Effectives
1	32	2,175
2	36	4,471
3	24	1,981
4	43	3,321

The Prussian cavalry which took part in the 1815 campaign comprised:

	Regiments	Squadrons
Hussars	9	33
Uhlans	8	–
Dragoons	5	19
Freiwillige Jäger Landwehr	12	–
Landwehr Cavalry	15	–
Total	49	

Prussian mounted officer, Foot Artillery of the Guard, 1809. Blue uniform with red piping around collar and cuffs. Red lining to jacket and stripe down overalls. Gold lace. From a contemporary print drawn by I. Wolf and engraved by F. Jügel.

At regimental and squadron level, cavalry tactics in Blücher's army were much the same as in those of his contemporaries. Their tasks may be summed up as reconnaissance and outpost duty on campaign, and mounted action as might be appropriate during a pitched battle.

In two ways the Prussian cavalry differed from Napoleon's. It had not a large body of heavy cavalry equipped with the cuirass. The other difference was that, while Napoleon kept a mass of reserve cavalry which was not affiliated to any *corps d'armée*, all the Prussian cavalry was distributed to the various corps. Napoleon's system, which permitted great strokes by a fully co-ordinated mounted arm upon the field of battle, was vastly superior.

Blücher was an inspiring leader, but not a clear-minded military thinker. It seems that he had not really thought out the best organization for his cavalry. Nor did he have any great cavalry commander at his disposal. Sohr and Henckel von Donnersmarck were first-class at the regimental level, but Blücher had nobody who could co-ordinate the movements of the cavalry as Uxbridge did for Wellington at Waterloo, and as Murat had done for Napoleon in the great days of the Empire.

Infantry

When Prussia took the field against Napoleon in 1813 she was desperately short of trained man-power. This was largely due to the restrictions laid down by the Treaty of Paris of 8 September 1808.

Strength of the Prussian Army including reserves: 1807, 53,523; 1808, 52,142; 1809, 45,897; 1810, 62,609; 1811, 74,553; 1812, 65,000.

Under a programme attributed to Scharnhorst there had been an attempt to train reserves. The success of the Krümper system has become part of Prussian legend, but the assertion that 150,000 reservists were available in 1813 rests only on the mistaken idea that the new units formed that year consisted entirely of reservists. That was not so; they were built on a nucleus of trained officers, NCOs and men, to which recruits were added.

That this was not easy is evident from the following figures:

Strength of the Prussian Army in June 1808:

	Infantry	Artillery	Cavalry	Total
Officers	1,079	147	535	1,761
NCOs	3,264	503	1,766	5,533
Musicians	659	35	199	893
Surgeons	227	27	86	340
Troops	10,025	2,161	5,651	17,837
Men on leave	17,396	1,653	4,634	23,683
Total	32,650	4,526	12,871	50,047

The Prussian Army, some 50,000 strong in 1808, comprised only 1,761 officers and 5,533 NCOs. There was a serious shortage of experienced officers and literate NCOs. On the other hand there was a source of potential officers in the Volunteers (*Freiwillige Jäger*), who came forward in substantial numbers.

The equipment left much to be desired. When 20,000 Austrian muskets were issued to the Silesian *Landwehr* it was discovered that the manufacturers had failed to bore touch-holes! Many of the soldiers had linen wallets instead of knapsacks.

Yorck, describing the state of his corps after Leipzig, tells us that of 106 guns he had in September only forty-two remained serviceable. Despite picking up a number of French muskets many of his men were unarmed:

'The troops who had taken part in the Russian campaign in Courtland were still wearing the clothing issued to them in 1811. The Silesian *Landwehr's* patrol jackets made out of coarse cloth had shrunk so badly as a result of wet bivouacs and rainy weather that they were too narrow fore and aft, and too short top and below. We were approaching a winter campaign and the men still had no cloth trousers. The adage about ten patches for one hole found widespread application on the tight-fitting coats.

'There was a great lack of shoes, although on the march from Leipzig any new or worn footwear to be found had been requisitioned. Many, and not only *Landwehr* men but also *Jäger* volunteers, marched barefooted. There was a shortage of cloaks too, but here and there people had taken them off prisoners. The horses for the artillery were worked very hard and many of them became unusable. What is more, the region we had marched through since leaving Halle was very poor in horses, so we had been able to requisition only a few.'

The spirit of the *Landwehr* sustained them even when they had to march without shoes. But the shortage of food, lack of straw and firewood, and generally indifferent administration took its toll. In the eighteen days ending 1 September 1813 Yorck's Corps dwindled from 37,000 to 25,300, the losses among the *Landwehr* far exceeding those of the line regiments.

The numbers of Regular and *Landwehr* infantry regiments in each corps were:

		1815			
	I	II	III	IV	*Total*
Regular	8	8	6	4	26
Landwehr	4	4	6	8	22
Total	12	12	12	12	48

Every Prussian regiment had two numbers, because they had a provincial as well as an army number. Thus the 21st was also the 4th Pomeranian Regiment, the 5th was also the 4th East Prussian, and so on.

The regiments were of three battalions, each of four companies. The first and second battalions were musketeers, the third was a fusilier battalion. The strength of a regiment was approximately sixty officers, 2,460 men and fifty-four musicians.

The infantry of the Prussian Army of 1806 fought in much the same style as the British Army of the same date – i.e. *before* the Peninsular War and the tactical improvements introduced by Sir John Moore and the Duke of Wellington. Both fought with their battalions in line, and met the French *tirailleurs* with a rather meagre proportion of light infantry. Nor is it strange that the two armies employed the same tactics since General Sir David Dundas (1735–1820), upon whose *Principles of military movements, chiefly applicable to infantry* (1788) most British infantry training was still based, had borrowed his ideas from the Prussian Army.

Blücher's men manoeuvred in much the same style as their French opponents, since with raw troops it was, generally speaking, much simpler to manoeuvre battalions and regiments in column. The men were not sufficiently well drilled to fight in line as Frederick's had done and Wellington's still did. The British relied primarily on fire-power in controlled volleys. The Prussians, at this period, believed in hand-to-hand fighting. Blücher, who, as we have seen, had no very high opinion of an officer who did not think that fighting man to man would solve practically any military problem, had managed to imbue his army with the same spirit.

If the Prussians lacked the iron discipline of Wellington's army we must remember that the majority of the rank and file were far less experienced. It is true that at Waterloo many of Wellington's troops saw action for the first time. But, even in the battalions that had not been in the Peninsula, the majority of the men had had five years' service. In consequence they were thoroughly well drilled, whereas the new Prussian army did not have this advantage.

The artillery was commanded by General von Holtzendorff, who was hit at Ligny. He was succeeded by Leutnant-Colonel von Röhl.

There were between thirty-eight and forty-one batteries. The foot and horse artillery batteries each had six guns and two howitzers. The siege-batteries each had eight howitzers.

There were approximately 174 6-pounders, fifty-

The Feldjäger *in the Prussian army wears the same style of uniform as the dragoon; the coat is green and has gold facings; the trousers grey with a red stripe.* (Roffe/Osprey)

Men of the Silesian rifle battalion wore green with black facings, red piping, and yellow metal buttons. The battalion acquired a fine reputation for endurance and gallantry in 1813 and 1814. (R. Knötel)

four 12-pounders, and ninety-two howitzers, making a total of 320 artillery pieces in all.

According to F. Bourdier there were only thirty-eight batteries:

Corps	Batteries	Guns	Men (including 492 pioneers)
I	11	88	1,258
II	10	80	1,575
III	6	48	1,062
IV	11	88	1,458
	38	304	5,353

These figures are based on those of the Belgian scholar, Winand Aerts, rather than the higher ones given by Major Becke.

To serve this formidable number of pieces there were only 4,861 artilleryman, and they had to be reinforced by infantrymen.

Blücher's army was not liberally provided with engineers and pioneers. In 1815 each of the four corps had one company of pioneers. They varied in strength from sixty-three with III Corps to 204 with I Corps.

The Elbe National Hussar Regiment. Green with grey overalls. The mounted hussar has gold lace and light blue collar and cuffs. In 1813 the Prussian provinces, East Prussia, Pomerania, and Silesia all raised National Cavalry Regiments. (R. Knötel)

Corps	Pioneers
I	204
II	74
III	63
IV	151
Total	492

Uniforms

A *Feldjäger* wore a green uniform, cut like that of a dragoon, with yellow facings and brass buttons. He had grey overalls trimmed with red, and black leather accoutrements, and had an oilskin cover to protect his shako. His sabre, which had a metal scabbard, was suspended from a waistbelt. The officers wore silver instead of yellow on their epaulette straps, and a silver sash as was usual in the Prussian service. In other respects there was little or no difference between the uniform or saddlery of officer and man. Shabracks, which were rather like those of the French hussars of the period, were trimmed with red.

The *Feldjäger* were a corps whose duties were similar to those of the Royal Staff Corps in the British service or the various troops of *Guides* in Napoleon's Army.

At this period Prussian hussar uniforms had much of the variety that one finds in the *Grande Armée*. A notable exception is that one does not find the *kolpak*, or busby, as worn by the *compagnie d'élite* in French hussar regiments.

In the 4th Silesian Regiment the dress of officers and men was very similar, though Bourdier's uniform plates show an NCO without the pelisse. Other ranks had silver instead of gold lace on their yellow collars, and their sashes were yellow and silver, alternately, as opposed to the silver of the officers. The sabretache was red with white trimmings and the shabrack was much the same as in the French service. A canteen was carried on the back of the saddle.

The Kolberg Infantry Regiment in 1811 wore a blue uniform with red facings and yellow metal buttons. These illustrations represent from left to right a grenadier, a musketeer, and a fusilier. (R. Knötel)

The Prussian privates depicted here belong to the 2nd Silesian Infantry Regiment. They wear uniforms of Prussian blue, with yellow collars and cuffs, a black shako with white-and-black Prussian pompom, and grey breeches with black gaiters.
(Gerry Embleton)

In theory, Silesian cavalry were supposed to have yellow collars and cuffs, but evidently stocks of yellow cloth were inadequate, and from the outset the 3rd and 4th Squadrons had red facings. Again, in theory, the buttons were supposed to be covered with red worsted. However, a sketch dated 19 June 1814 showed red collars and yellow metal buttons. It is as well to be reminded from time to time that regiments do not always conform to the Dress Regulations, especially in armies which are raised at short notice!

In the Prussian service it seems that the trumpeters wore a uniform of the same colour as the rest of the regiment, their normal distinction being the special form of epaulette.

Sky-blue and green appear to have been the main colours of the Prussian dragoon uniforms. There were two quite distinctive styles of coat or jacket, the *litewka* and *kollet*.

The 5th Brandenburg Regiment had sky blue cloth shabracks with a black edging. The portmanteau was grey and the canteen was slung at the back of the saddle on the left side. This was the normal arrangement among the dragoons, the shabrack and its trimmings following the colours of the coat and its facings.

Uhlans and Staff
Generally speaking, the uniform of Prussian uhlans resembled that of the Polish Lancers in Napoleon's Army. For the most part, officers and men wore the

Prussian dragoons triumphantly carrying off a Russian colour at the Battle of Eckau. (From a watercolour by R. Knötel)

Blücher nearly loses his life at the Battle of Ligny. He is trapped under his dead horse and only his ADC remains to defend him. (Print by Wolf and von Maner)

Field Marshal G. L. von Blücher. He was also Prince of Wahlstadt. His reputation is somewhat overshadowed by that of Napoleon and Wellington but he was an outstanding general. (Engraving by G. Kruell)

czapska, a short jacket, and overalls. The *litewka*, though found in Lützow's Corps, was unusual. Instead of the *czapska* some regiments, which had formerly been hussars, retained their shakos.

Line Infantry

The infantry of the line wore a shako, a short jacket – those of the officers had rather longer tails – breeches, and gaiters. An occasional variation was white trousers. Prussian blue was the dominant colour, but

The general on the Prussian Staff shows distinctive collars and cuffs to his litewka, *as well as epaulettes. His sash is silver, as was usual for Prussian service.* (Roffe/Osprey)

Prussian volunteers setting off for the wars. The father is proud, the mother and daughter are tearful, and the younger brother is glumly envious.

the Silesian Jäger wore green as one would expect, and grey and even black were sometimes found. Breeches were usually grey, and boots or gaiters black. Silesian infantry wore a black shako with a white band round the top, bearing the white-and-black Prussian pompom in front. The coat was Prussian blue and had a yellow collar and cuffs: the shoulder-straps and the turn-backs to the coat-tails were scarlet, and the cuff-slashes (the vertical strips of cloth on the cuff) were the same colour as the coat. The buttons on the front of the coat, on the shoulder-straps, and on the cuff-slashes were brass. Grey breeches were worn with black gaiters. The greatcoat was rolled round the body when on campaign, with a strip of brown leather to keep it tidy: he carried a white knapsack on his hip for rations, and he would also have a mess-tin encased in a white canvas cover attached to the back of his pack by a leather strap. His sword was carried in a brown leather scabbard with a brass tip; the drum of the regimental drummer was suspended from a white leather belt bearing a brass plate with two sockets into which the drumsticks are thrust when not in use.

The Officer of Fusiliers would have a band of gold braid round his shako with gilt eagles and a gilt chain. As decoration, the black-and-silver cockade would have a gold-braided loop and button, above which was a silver pompom with black centre. The shoulder-straps to his coat were red trimmed with silver braid, and he carried a grey goatskin pack slung from white straps. The sword-scabbard was trimmed in gilt and the sword had a gilt hilt with a silver sword-knot. The waist-sash was silver with two rows of black threads running through it.

Most of the *Landwehr* cavalry wore the *litewka* and were armed with the lance.

The resemblance of the uniform to some of the Polish Lancers of the *Grande Armée de Varsovie* was remarkable. Bourdier showed a trooper of the same regiment with an oilskin cover over his *czapska* and with a yellow and red lance pennon. The shabrack was blue with yellow trimmings.

In 1806 the Prussian Noble Guard decide to sharpen their swords on the steps of the French Embassy in Berlin, with suitable accompanying gestures. (Watercolour by E. de Myrbach)

The appearance of the *Landwehr* Infantry was rather more casual than that of the line. The *litewka* seems to have been a popular garment; while both officers and men wore trousers instead of breeches and gaiters. Headgear varied from a cap, often with an oilskin cover, such as Blücher himself favoured, to a shako like that of the regulars. Some of the shakos were probably of British origin.

The uniforms of the Prussian artillery were not all of Prussian blue with grey trousers. Those of Lützow's Corps wore a black *litewka*; the Russo-German Legion wore a short green jacket with black collar and cuffs, and red piping.

The cannoneer, Silesian Brigade had collar and cuffs of a different colour from the epaulette straps. The explanation is that the latter were of the Silesian colour: yellow. The Brandenburg Brigade had red epaulette straps.

The Silesian Rifle Battalion uniform was green. The facings were black with red piping. From 1809 to 1812 the battalion was in garrison at Lieguitz; it was formed in 1808 from a number of light companies which had defended Glatz in 1807. In 1813 it took part in a great deal of fighting, notably at Kulen, where it took two French colours. At Vauchamps in 1814 two of its companies showed their strength in repulsing a superior force of the cavalry of Napoleon's guard. In 1815 the Silesian Rifles served in Zieten's (I) Corps.

4
EXPATRIATE CORPS

The King's German Legion

The King's German Legion came into existence as a result of the overrunning of the Electorate of Hanover by General Mortier, at the head of 13,000 Frenchmen, in 1803. The Hanoverians had been ill-prepared for the blow, though large French armies had been close to her borders for some time. Forces to repel the invader had been allowed to run down, along with the fortresses that could have drawn off the attack. The situation had been dangerous for the inhabitants since the Prussians had occupied the Electorate in 1801; morale was low, the army consisted of 15,546 men, mainly cavalry, infantry, artillery, and engineers, but over a third of these were on more or less permanent leave.

In May 1803, Talleyrand (the French Foreign Minister) had informed the British Ambassador that unless British rearmament ceased forthwith, the First Consul would be forced to send 20,000 men to Holland and, as Hanover was near by, it was 'natural' that they would make up a camp on the Electorate's borders.

The Prime Minister of Hanover, von Lenthe, refused to take any action upon receiving news of this clear threat. Finally the Hanoverian forces were mobilized under Field Marshal Wallmoden, but received no assistance from von Lenthe's government.

Major van der Decken of the Hanoverian army was sent secretly to Berlin to enlist Prussian aid for the Anglo-Hanoverian cause, but without success. Russia then informed Prussia that if Prussian troops occupied Hanover again, Russia would take this as an act of war against herself and would react accordingly.

The Duke of Brunswick, commander-in-chief of the armies of the Holy Roman Empire (or German Confederation) refused a Hanoverian request for aid in the case of a French attack and Hanover was thus left very much on her own.

For an unexplained reason, the Hanoverian intelligence of the opposing French army was very bad; the potential invaders consisted of not more than 13,000 men, badly equipped and completely without artillery and with only a few poorly-mounted squadrons of cavalry; the Hanoverian rumour increased this force to 30,000 men.

On 1 June 1803 the Duke of Cambridge assumed command of the 4,000 strong Hanoverian forces assembled at Nienburg. Total mobilized Hanoverian forces were 2,700 cavalry and 6,300 infantry. The French, under General Mortier, invaded Hanover and were met by a deputation sent by the Hanoverian government who agreed that the Hanoverian army would not take up arms against the French in the forthcoming war. The Duke of Cambridge, learning of this, left at once for England in disgust.

The dithering and dallying of the Hanoverian government continued as did Mortier's advance and on 2 June 1803 there was the first clash of the campaign at the village of Borstel where the French, after having taken prisoner a Hanoverian officer and trumpeter (who had advanced under a flag of truce), were checked by Hanoverian cavalry. The 9th and 10th Hanoverian Dragoons, a company of light infantry and two guns threw the French back. This was to be the only clash of the 1803 campaign.

General von Hammerstein, commanding the Hanoverian advanced guard, now withdrew over the River Weser because he felt himself too weak to

A rear view of a dolman of an officer in the Horse Artillery. It was originally dark blue in colour but has now faded to dark green. (Bomann Museum, Celle)

remain west of that obstacle in the face of the larger French force.

On 3 June the Convention of Suhlingen was signed between the Hanoverian deputies (von Bremer, a court official, and *Oberstleutnant* von Bock, commander of the Leibgarde-Regiment) and Mortier.

This Convention demanded that the Hanoverian army should withdraw east over the River Elbe and deliver up its artillery to the French. This was done.

On 15 June news was received that Napoleon had refused to accept the Suhlingen Convention and that hostilities were to recommence. Thus, by a series of tricks and bluffs, the French were now in possession of almost all of Hanover at the cost of one minor cavalry skirmish.

Plans were prepared in England to send ships to the Elbe to bring out the Hanoverian army but events overtook these plans.

A second Convention was now prepared by General Alexander Berthier, Napoleon's Chief of Staff; it was short:

1   The Hanoverian troops will withdraw over the Elbe, lay down their weapons and be taken to France. They will retain all their baggage, the officers their swords, and the latter may choose a place of residence on the Continent but may not go to England.
2   The Hanoverian Army may march past with all the honours of war. Arrangements will be made for the feeding of the men and the transport of the baggage.
3   This capitulation shall be valid without requiring the ratification of either government.

Von Lenthe had already warned Wallmoden to accept these terms. At this point Wallmoden commanded 2,000 cavalry, 7,000 infantry, and fifty 3-pounder 'Amusettes' of light regimental artillery, and some howitzers. They were cut off from all sources of reinforcement or supply, and the howitzers had been permitted him by the French general as *pièces d'honneur*. His ammunition would last for two days' action at normal rates. Mortier had 13,000 men, but his logistical situation was vastly better than his opponent's.

Wallmoden called a council of war and it was decided to fight but before action occurred, von Lenthe arrived at his headquarters bearing a new, revised Capitulation which held better terms. The fight was delayed, morale slumped, the men became uneasy and the moment for action slipped away.

It was finally arranged that Wallmoden and Mortier should meet in a boat anchored in the middle of the River Elbe to sign the revised Convention and this was done on 5 July 1803 near the village of Artlenburg. Under the terms of this treaty the Hanoverian army was disbanded.

King George III refused to ratify the Elbe Convention. He inherited as King of England the title of Elector of Hanover, since the line of the house of Welfen, Hanover's traditional rulers, came to England through George I in 1714. With the union between Britain and Hanover, the army owed its allegiance to the English monarch. Without George III's assent the third clause in the Convention

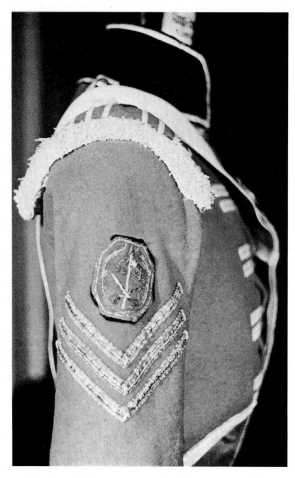

This part-uniform of a colour-sergeant in the 7th Line Battalion is preserved in the Bomann museum. The colours are now faded but it is possible to pick out everything except some of the woven detail.

The discovery of this well-preserved tunic of a Grenadier company sergeant settled a controversy about the colour of the turnbacks, which, in fact, were white. (Bomann Museum, Celle)

had no effect, and the Hanoverians were enabled to fight against France.

By 28 July 1803 von der Decken (who had now been promoted to lieutenant-colonel) was in England and had secured letters patent from the king to raise a 'King's German Regiment' formed of foreigners including ex-members of the Hanoverian Army. Its strength was not to exceed 4,000 men.

Due to von der Decken's personal unpopularity in Hanoverian circles and the fact that many potential recruits were deterred from joining because they feared that, once in English uniform, they would be shipped off to one of the far-flung colonies to die of yellow fever or some other plague, recruits were

initially slow in coming forward.

There was a conditional clause in von der Decken's patent: if the corps had not reached a strength of 400 within three months it would be disbanded.

The recruits came in a thin trickle until the end of September 1803, and even this trickle was admirable considering the obstacles and perils which recruiters and recruits had to overcome in Hanover.

The first depot of the regiment in England was at Lymington near Southampton, but this was soon too small and they were moved to the Isle of Wight. Major von Hinüber, who had already distinguished himself in British service in India, became the first commander on 13 October 1803 on the Isle of Wight.

Marshal Soult. The Legion fought against him on several occasions and accounted him a formidable adversary. The English called him 'The Duke of Damnation', which was one way of expressing his title 'Duc de Dalmatie'.

This trooper in the 2nd Light Dragoons is in Field Service Dress. He wears white buttons and epaulettes; if he were an officer these would be silver. The 1st Light Dragoons had yellow buttons and epaulettes. He carries a curved light-cavalry sabre. (Roffe/Osprey)

The French meanwhile had not been idle in occupied Hanover. As well as hindering the recruitment for the 'King's German Reigment', they were actively canvassing for their own 'Légion Hannovrien'. Only three former officers of the Hanoverian army joined this Legion (a lieutenant and two ensigns) and one of these was a Danish subject by birth, so unsuccessful was it. The *Légion Hannovrien* consisted of infantry (clothed in red with dark blue facings) and cavalry (dark green with yellow facings). Apart from Hanoverians, its 1,400 men included a large majority from many other nations; it was disbanded in 1811, its members going into the 127th French Line Infantry Regiment which was recruited from Germans in and around Hamburg.

The Organization of the Legion
On the same day that von der Decken received his patent to raise the King's German Regiment, a Scottish officer (recently out of Dutch service) Major Colin Halkett, was given permission to raise a similar foreign corps for English service. It was to be a battalion of 459 men initially but if he succeeded in increasing it to 800 men he was to be promoted lieutenant-colonel.

On 3 October 1803 the King's German Regiment had 450 men and its future was thus secure. In fact, things looked so promising that the original patent was extended to embrace a corps of all arms (cavalry, artillery, engineers and infantry) whose strength was not to exceed 5,000 men.

Former members of the Hanoverian army were now streaming into England via Heligoland and thus

Murat, King of Naples. He tried to invade Italy in 1810 but was repulsed in actions in which three battalions of the Legion distinguished themselves.

the training of specialists, such as artillerymen, was no problem.

In mid-November 1803 the King's German Regiment was moved from the Isle of Wight to Hilsea Barracks, Portsmouth (a camp which in 1952 still held British soldiers). Their strength now was about

Lieut-General Julius Hartman who commanded the Royal Hanoverian Artillery and Engineers. He fought at Waterloo.

This is the cap-plate of a Line Battalion of the Legion. The battalion number is in the centre, surrounded by the Legion's title.

A belt-plate from a Line Battalion of the Legion dating from the period 1803 to 1816.

1,000 men and they were organized into two light infantry battalions and a battalion of line infantry. Cadres for the horse artillery and cavalry were training separately in Weymouth, the foot artillery were in Hilsea Barracks. By the end of 1803 one horse and one foot battery had been formed. The cavalry

This illuminated scroll was produced to mark the fiftieth anniversary of the fight at Garcia-Hernandez in July 1812. The 1st and 2nd Heavy Dragoons of the Legion broke two fully-formed French infantry squares. This would have been a fine feat at any period but was particularly with such seasoned opponents.

were organized into four squadrons of heavy and four of light dragoons and by February 1804 each arm was increased to six squadrons of 450 sabres. Living in Weymouth and Dorchester and commanded by Major-General von Linsingen, they were popular with the king who often appeared in the uniform of the heavy dragoons.

On 19 December 1803 the King's German Regiment had been combined with Halkett's foreign corps and was henceforth known as the 'King's German Legion'. The overall command of the Legion was given to Adolph, Duke of Cambridge who was very popular with the Hanoverians due to his previous connexion with them.

During its existence over 15,000 men entered the King's German Legion and of these 75.5% were Hanoverians (42% were members of the old Electoral army), 17% were Germans of other states, and only 7.5% were 'foreigners'. The artillery and cavalry in particular were almost purely Hanoverian while the two light battalions contained the highest percentage of 'foreigners'.

In April 1804 the 2nd Line Infantry Battalion of the Legion was raised, and in May the 3rd. The 2nd Foot Artillery Battery was completed in July and the formation of a second horse artillery and third foot artillery battery was begun.

By January 1805 the King's German Legion consisted of the following units:

CAVALRY BRIGADE
Major General von Linsingen
1st Regiment of Heavy Dragoons – Colonel von Bock
1st Regiment of Light Dragoons (Hussars) –
Colonel Viktor von Alten

LIGHT INFANTRY BRIGADE
Colonel von Alten
1st Light Battalion – commanded by the brigadier
2nd Light Battalion – Lieutenant-Colonel Halkett

FIRST LINE BRIGADE
Colonel von Barsse
1st Line Battalion – Colonel von Ompteda
2nd Line Battalion – commanded by the brigadier

SECOND LINE BRIGADE
Colonel von Langworth
3rd Line Battalion – Colonel von Hinüber
4th Line Battalion – commanded by the brigadier

ARTILLERY
Commander – Colonel von der Decken (also
Adjutant-general of the Legion)
Major Friedrich von Linsingen
1st Horse Artillery Battery – Captain
G. J. Hartmann
2nd Horse Artillery Battery – Captain Röttiger
1st Horse Artillery Battery – Captain Brückmann
2nd Foot Artillery Battery – Captain Kuhlmann
3rd Foot Artillery Battery – Captain Heise

ENGINEERS
Captains Berensbach, Prott and Meinecke
Lieutenants Hassebroik, Appuhn and Schweitzer

For internal use, drill commands were given in

This officer in the 1st Hussars is wearing parade dress. Hussars were light cavalry and derive their name from the 'huszar' – a Hungarian light horseman. He wears a brown busby with no peak, a dark blue dolman and pelisse, and a crimson sash with gold barrels. (Roffe/Osprey)

This officer in the 2nd Hussars wears two gold buttons and laces on each side of the dolman collar. They also had black sheepskin saddle-rugs as a form of cloak for wear on other occasions than parades. (Roffe/Osprey)

German; English being used only on large parades and manoeuvres.

In July 1805 at Weymouth, the Cavalry Brigade and Captain Hartmann's horse artillery battery were part of an 8,000 strong corps in an exercise camp under command of the Duke of Cumberland. The

Germans were by no means behind the English when it came to demonstrating martial skills.

In February 1806, in north Hanover, the 2nd Heavy Dragoons and the 3rd Light Dragoons were raised; each about 500 strong, and the 2nd Light Dragoons were brought up to the same strength. Each existing infantry battalion was increased to 1,000 strong and 5th, 6th and 7th Line Battalions were formed.

Three hundred men were engaged to form the cadre of the 8th Line Battalion and a 4th Foot Battery was raised for the artillery. In mid-February 1806 the expeditionary force was re-embarked from Hanover and returned to Southampton where the cavalry, the three newly-raised infantry battalions and the artillery disembarked. The two light battalions and the 1st, 2nd, 3rd, and 4th Line Battalions sailed on to Ireland. They were followed in April by the 1st Heavy and the 1st Light Dragoons who embarked in Liverpool for Dublin.

The 2nd Heavy Dragoons went to Northampton under Colonel von Veltheim; the 2nd Light Dragoons were in Canterbury under Colonel Viktor von Alten. The 3rd Light Dragoons, under Colonel von Roden, were in Guildford. All the cavalry of the Legion were mounted on English horses even though many Hanoverian horses had been bought in the Electorate during the expedition. The 5th and 6th Infantry Battalions formed the 3rd Line Brigade under Colonel Dreiberg and were posted to Winchester where they were joined in May by the 4th Line Brigade (7th and 8th Line Battalions) under Major-General von Drechsel. The artillery was in Porchester commanded by Major Röttiger.

A word here to the status of the Legion in relation to the British Army; although the officers of the Legion received their commissions from George III, they were not part of the British Army and were considered inferior to British officers in that they belonged to a 'foreign corps'.

The 1st Line Brigade was soon moved from Ireland to Gibraltar, which place they reached at the end of June 1806. The 3rd Line Brigade took their place in Ireland.

Artillery

The Regimental staff: One colonel-commander, one lieutenant-colonel, two majors, two adjutants, one quartermaster (QM), one paymaster, five surgeons, one veterinary surgeon.

The junior staff: One sergeant-major, one quartermaster-sergeant (RQMS), one paymaster-sergeant.

Apart from these there were the captain-commissary and the schoolmaster (for the soldiers' children).

Each horse artillery battery had: One captain 1st Class, one captain 2nd Class, two lieutenants, two 2nd lieutenants, one battery-sergeant-major (BSM), one battery-quartermaster-sergeant (BQMS), three sergeants, four corporals, seven bombardiers, one trumpeter, ninety gunners, one farrier, two blacksmiths, two collarmakers (for repairing harness), two wheelwrights.

The train: One sergeant, two corporals, one trumpeter, fifty-seven drivers.

The artillery pieces in each horse artillery battery were: five 6-pounder cannon, each drawn by six horses; one $5\frac{1}{2}$-inch howitzer drawn by eight horses.

The foot batteries (both 6- and 9-pounder) had the same six officers as the horse batteries but only three sergeants and, as long as the battery was static, two drummers who converted to mounted trumpeters when the battery was on the move.

Other mounted personnel were the officers, six non-commissioned officers (NCOs), the train and the blacksmith.

The foot batteries had four guns and two $5\frac{1}{2}$-inch howitzers, and the 9-pounder battery was stronger than the 6-pounder by three bombardiers, four gunners, thirty-nine drivers and one blacksmith. It also had four guns and two $5\frac{1}{2}$-inch howitzers.

Ammunition wagons and the smith's field forge were drawn by six horses each, the other vehicles by four horses, and the reserve gun carriages by two horses.

Each battery had eight ammunition wagons, two baggage wagons, and one field forge. In addition there was a further wagon of small arms ammunition and the reserve horses.

The gun-carriages were lighter than those of the rest of the British Army and thus more manoeuvrable, which was a considerable advantage in the Peninsular campaign.

The limbers initially were two-wheelers with seats for the unmounted members of the battery, but in 1807 they were replaced by limbers which also towed the gun, and seats were also provided on these.

Cavalry

A regiment consisted of: one colonel-commander, two majors (one of which became a lieutenant-colonel), one adjutant, one paymaster, three surgeons, one veterinary surgeon, one regimental-sergeant-major (RSM), one paymaster-sergeant, one saddler, one armourer, one farrier.

Each troop contained: one captain, one lieutenant, one cornet, one quartermaster, four sergeants, four corporals, one trumpeter, seventy-six troopers.

On 24 June 1809 a quartermaster of officer's rank was introduced for the whole regiment and the non-commissioned troop QMs were abolished.

The troops were distinguished by the letters A, B, C, etc. and the squadrons by numbers 1–5. The troops and squadrons were organized as follows:

1 Squadron – A and F Troops
2 Squadron – B and G Troops
3 Squadron – C and H Troops
4 Squadron – D and I Troops
5 Squadron – E and K Troops

Infantry

Regimental staff (the term regiment was used even though it was in fact a battalion): one colonel-commander, one lieutenant-colonel, two majors, one adjutant, one auditor, one quartermaster, three surgeons, one RSM, one regimental-auditor-sergeant, one RQMS, one armourer.

Each company consisted of: one captain, two lieutenants, one ensign, five sergeants, five corporals (one of which was the company-quartermaster), one drummer/bugler (line/light battalion), ninety-six privates (two of whom were drummers/trumpeters), one pioneer.

The companies were distinguished alphabetically within each battalion.

The Garrison Company (25 March 1805)

One captain, two lieutenants, one ensign, five sergeants, five corporals, two drummers, ninety-five privates.

In December 1806 this was reduced to: one lieutenant, one sergeant, two corporals, forty-eight privates.

Horses

Dragoons' horses were from fourteen hands one inch to sixteen hands two inches tall; hussars' horses were from fourteen hands one inch to fifteen hands two inches. (Nowadays, horses below fourteen hands two inches high are considered to be 'ponies'.)

Price limits for buying dragoon and hussar mounts were thirty guineas and twenty-five guineas respectively.

Colouring was mixed, but greys were used only by the musicians and trumpeters.

Tails were cropped as was the English fashion of the day and each horse had a name beginning with the initial letter of the troop to which it belonged.

Training

The German officers, then as now, had a much more earnest approach to soldiering than their English counterparts and the standard of training of the King's German Legion was considerably higher than that of normal English line regiments. For example, in the Legion, the officers used to drill their men; a task left to their NCOs by most English officers.

Initially, drill and commands were on the old Hanoverian model and German was used. English superseded this in the artillery and cavalry in 1807, later than in the Line Battalions. The two Light Battalions retained their German customs to the end, but English drill was used in parades and guard-mounting.

The Legion also absorbed many English sports such as cricket, football, boxing, rowing, quarter-staff fighting, etc. The officers adopted the English custom of foxhunting which they also enjoyed during the Peninsular campaign.

Tactical Cavalry Formations

Cavalry formed in two ranks with four feet distance between them. The squadron was divided into four divisions and was commanded by the senior captain. Each lieutenant commanded a troop and positioned himself on the outer wing. The cornets were in the centre of the squadron. All officers were shadowed by NCOs who took their places in their absence.

The second captain and the senior cornet commanded in the centre of the second rank.

The march was mostly at the trot, the charge at the gallop with four paces distance between the ranks.

Skirmishers pushed out 300–400 paces from the main body at twenty-five-pace intervals along the front. In this formation, the second rank of the main body was ten paces behind and to the left of the first.

When engaging the enemy, the first rank would have their sabres hanging from the sword-knots on their wrists and would engage the enemy with pistol or carbine according to range; the second rank drew and held only their sabres.

Tactical Infantry Formations
Companies consisted of two platoons each of two sections and were arranged in line precedence (according to the seniority of their officers) from right to left. With the introduction of ten companies per battalion in 1812 (including a grenadier and a light company), this system became inoperative as the grenadier company was always on the right and the light company always on the left of the battalion line.

Sharpshooters (a Hanoverian custom) were used in front of the battalion when in action. These sharp-shooters were picked marksmen who carried rifles and wore distinguishing items of uniform. They consisted of a subaltern, four sergeants, a bugler and fifty-two men per battalion. In action they formed into two detachments on the flanks and to the rear of the main body of the battalion. Sometimes all sharpshooters of a brigade would be collected together under a captain.

This policy was sometimes applied to the light companies as well but very rarely to the grenadier companies.

The battle-line was a double rank (since 1804) with two feet six inches between ranks; in order to fire, the second rank moved six inches forwards and to the right, thus moving into the spaces between their comrades in the front rank.

On parade the battalion commander and the adjutants were in the front centre of the battalion; captains on the right wings of their companies, other officers three paces to the rear of the second rank.

The famous square (a formation used to guard against attack by cavalry) was hollow and of three or four ranks depth along each face; the outer two ranks would kneel.

Bayonets were normally carried fixed by the line battalions, but the light battalions fixed them only when specifically ordered.

Before closing with the enemy, a salvo would be fired; line battalions then attacked at a speed of seventy-five paces to the minute and light battalions at 108 paces. On the command 'Charge', the first

rank went into the 'on guard' position and the second rank shouldered arms; a 'Hurrah' was given and contact made.

Movements were mostly made in open columns of divisions but closed column was used in action.

Column marches were carried out in four ranks, but in Spain the narrow tracks forced the use of a three-abreast formation.

When fire-fighting with the enemy, the second rank would move forward past the first rank to fire and then retire again to load. Signals were given by whistle.

On parades and reviews a march past at seventy-five paces per minute was first performed, with all officers dismounted; a second march past in quick time with officers mounted then followed. Officers when mounted, saluted with the drawn sword only because the left hand held the reins, but with drawn sword and by raising the left hand to the headdress when on foot. Other ranks always carried their arms shouldered.

Uniforms
Apart from minor appointments, the Legion was dressed exactly as their British counterparts. These minor differences consisted of various initials and titles worn on cap-plates, belt-plates, buttons, turnbacks, packs, and canteens.

Knötel, in his plate 24, Volume III of the series *Uniformenkunde*, shows the line battalions of the Legion with blue turnbacks to the skirts of their jackets and blue fields to the wings of the flank companies. In the notes to this plate Knötel states that in Beamish and von Brandis the turnbacks are white as for the British line infantry but that he has shown them blue because they appear so in *Costumes of the Army of the British Empire 1814*.

All the Legion line infantry jackets in the Bomann museum in Celle and in the Hanover musuem show white turnbacks and *Costumes of the British Empire 1814* is the only source which differs. (No picture has been found of the Legion infantry in the 'stovepipe' shako worn in the British Army from 1800 to 1812.)

Coats of generals, staff officers, engineer officers, and line infantry officers were long-skirted (changed to short-skirted in 1812). Other ranks' coats were always short-skirted.

Facing colours on collars, cuffs, and officers' lapels were dark blue for line infantry officers, black for

Officer, 1st Light Battalion, field service uniform. Unlike their men, officers wore no cap-badges on their shakos. (Roffe/Osprey)

Bugler of sharpshooters of a line battalion. He would probably not carry his rifle in action, as his task was to give commands with his bugle. (Roffe/Osprey)

engineers. Turnbacks were white for staff officers, generals, and officers of the line battalions; collars and cuffs were blue.

Artillery coats were initially a short-skirted dark blue coat with red collar, cuffs, and turnbacks. Later,

however, the mounted batteries of the Legion adopted the blue dolman which the Royal Horse Artillery also had (and retain for ceremonial wear for King's Troop, RHA to this day).

Heavy dragoon regiments : scarlet coat with long skirts initially, later short. Facings on collar, cuffs, and turnbacks: 1st Regiment – dark blue, 2nd Regiment – black. Lace and buttons were yellow.

On 25 December 1813 they became light dragoon regiments wearing dark blue kolletts with red lapels, cuffs, turnbacks, and collars. Other ranks only received this uniform for the 1815 campaign.

Hussars : The 1st Regiment wore the same uniform as the old 9th Hanoverian Cavalry Regiment of 1803; a blue kollett with red facings and yellow lace and buttons. The other two regiments wore the normal British light dragoon uniform which later was of the hussar type. Initially they wore only a dolman but the 3rd regiment wore red-lined pelisses from their formation and the other two regiments soon imitated them.

Facings : 1st Regiment – scarlet collar and cuffs; yellow lace and buttons.

2nd Regiment – white collar and cuffs; yellow lace and buttons.

3rd Regiment – yellow collar and cuffs; white lace and buttons.

Fur on the pelisses was black for the 1st Regiment, white for the 2nd, and in the 3rd Regiment Knötel shows an officer in black fur and a hussar in grey in 1813.

The light battalions had a far more individualistic uniform; the 1st Battalion had lighter green uniforms than the 2nd, collars and cuffs were black for both, but uniform cut varied also. The 1st Battalion had a jacket with very short skirts, whereas the 2nd Battalion wore a dolman (officers had black silk lacing on the chest which other ranks did not have) with three rows of buttons.

Generals and line battalion officers' coats were double-breasted; the men's single-breasted.

Button designs included the King's cipher, a crown, crossed sabres, a bugle, the name of the Legion in a garter form, and the initials of the unit without the garter.

Buttons were gold for generals, the staff, engineers, artillery, both Heavy and the 1st Light Dragoons, and the line battalions; white for the 3rd Hussars and the light battalions.

Gold embroidery was sewn on to the collars, cuffs, and breasts of the jackets of the generals, the staff and officers of engineers, artillery, heavy dragoons, and infantry. The men's jackets were bordered with a white lace. Headgear was, for officers, mostly the black bicorn, with black cockade and a white over red plume. This was worn sideways in peacetime but in action worn fore and aft and with brass chin-scales. The tips of the bicorn almost reached the wearer's shoulders.

In 1811 the shako was introduced for officers of the foot artillery batteries, while the horse artillery officers wore the crested, British light dragoon helmet.

The officers and men of the heavy dragoons wore iron cross-pieces under their bicorns in action; these metal skullguards were called 'Secrets'.

As from March 1812, line infantry officers adopted the '1812' (or Waterloo) pattern shako for duty wear. The light dragoons also wore a shako (but of a different pattern from that of the infantry) on their conversion from heavy dragoons, and the 1st and 2nd Hussars initially wore this headgear also, but the 3rd Regiment wore a busby of black fur with a red bag. This was rapidly copied by the other two regiments.

All ranks of the 1st Light Battalion wore a black conical shako, officers of the 2nd a 'Winged cap' (*'Flügelmütze'* or 'Mirliton'); the men wore the conical shako.

Generals and staff officers wore white breeches and Hessian boots with spurs screwed in. Engineer officers wore grey trousers with a gold stripe; foot artillery officers, grey with a red stripe, and other ranks of foot artillery, grey trousers without stripes, black lace shoes, and black leather gaiters into which the trousers were sometimes put. Horse artillery on parade wore white breeches and Hessian boots with buckle-on spurs, while the heavy dragoons wore the higher, cuffed boots and white breeches.

The 1st Hussars wore blue overalls with silver stripes (other ranks without stripes), the 2nd and 3rd Hussars wore grey overalls with a gold stripe for officers (no stripe for other ranks).

Line infantry officers wore grey trousers with silver stripes, and infantry other ranks wore the same shoes and gaiters as the foot artillery.

Greatcoats for mounted troops were dark blue with large cape collars; for the dismounted arms, grey with no cape collar.

Badges of Rank

a. *Generals :* Aiguilettes, gold chevrons on the lower arm and gold embroidery on cuffs, collars and chests.

b. *Officers*: (except hussars and light battalion officers who wore no distinguishing marks): Gold epaulettes with thick or thin fringes on both shoulders down through major. Captains – one gold epaulette on the right shoulder. Lieutenants – 'wings', of yellow or white scales on both shoulders.

c. Other ranks: chevrons on the right upper arm.

Sergeant-major	– four and a crown
Sergeant	– three
Corporal and cadet	– two
Lance-corporal	– one

Almost all officers wore waist sashes which were gold and crimson silk for generals and crimson silk for all other officers. Sergeant-majors also had red worsted waist sashes and also wore double-breasted jackets. Sergeants wore red worsted sashes with a central stripe in the facing colour.

The hussars and the 2nd Light Battalion wore hussar-type barrel sashes and the light dragoons a *Pass gurtel* or 'stable-belt'.

For fatigues the men wore a blue cloth cap, white waistcoat, and drill trousers. Each Commanding Officer controlled his own regiment's fatigue dress.

Officers could also please themselves largely what they wore in camp; hats, trousers and boots were 'to taste'. For generals and staff officers there was a simple blue uniform without aiguilettes or embroidery.

Badges were also stamped on shoulder-belt plates.

Weapons

The Artillery: Foot batteries used 12- and 6-pounder guns and $5\frac{1}{2}$-inch howitzers.

Horse batteries used 3-pounder guns and $5\frac{1}{2}$-inch howitzers.

Barrel dimensions were:

	Weight	Length	Calibre	Normal charge of Powder
The 6-pounder	$5\frac{1}{2}$ cwt	5 ft	3.5 in	$1\frac{1}{2}$ lb
The 9-pounder	$13\frac{1}{4}$ cwt	6 ft	4 in	3 lb
The (15-pounder) $5\frac{1}{2}$-inch howitzer	13 cwt	4 ft 8 in	$5\frac{1}{2}$ in	$2\frac{1}{2}$ lb

The 9-pounder replaced the 12-pounder which was too heavy for good mobility in the field.

Personal Weapons

Horse Artillery

Officers: curved sabres in steel scabbards on a black sling belt; crimson and gold sword-knot; black sabretache, white leather bandolier (gold for parades), and pouch.

Other ranks: white sabre belt over the right shoulder, sabre with white leather fist-strap, pistol in white holster with ammunition-pouch attached.

Foot Artillery

Officers: sabres on white slings.

Other ranks: a white shoulder belt on right shoulder carrying a short '*Hirshfänger*' in leather scabbard. In addition six carbines were carried in clips on the limbers and each gunner had an ammunition pouch on his waistbelt.

Cavalry

Officers of heavy dragoons had the heavy, straight sword with fist-guard of that arm in a steel scabbard on black slings. Other ranks had the same weapon on white slings, a carbine and a pistol.

When these two regiments were converted to light dragoons in 1813, they were rearmed as the hussars, i.e. curved sabre, with a single bar fist-guard in a steel scabbard on black slings; two pistols and a carbine.

All cavalry carried black sabretaches and wore white bandoliers. Officers on parade wore silver or gold bandoliers and steel pouches. The officers of hussars had embroidered red cloth sabretaches. All officers and other ranks wore sword-knots as for the horse artillery.

The pistols were more for signalling than fighting; they had no sights and their maximum range was fifty paces. Carbines reached to 180 paces, were smooth-bored, and were inferior to the French model. Up to the time of the Peninsular War, the heavy dragoons carried a bayonet for their carbines.

Carbines hung from a clip on the bandolier with the muzzle, on the march, laid on the right holster-cover and, when ready for action, in a boot behind the right heel of the rider.

Carbines had the same calibre as the pistol, thirty balls were carried in the pouch, the ball weighed $1\frac{1}{3}$ oz, and a normal powder charge was $\frac{3}{8}$ oz.

Infantry Weapons

Normal line infantry had the famous British Brown

Bess smooth-bore musket; sharpshooters and light battalions used the Baker rifled musket for one-third of their number, the other two-thirds using smooth bores as for the line. Two calibres were thus used. The 'Brown Bess' musket fired a 2 oz. ball with a powder charge of $\frac{5}{8}$ oz. It was 4 ft $9\frac{1}{3}$ in. long.

Officers of light battalions carried the hussar sabre and wore a bandolier with signal whistle. NCOs also had bandoliers and whistles.

Light battalion, other ranks, carried bayonets or *Hirschfänger* (according to the weapon they fired) in leather scabbards on their waistbelts.

Line infantry other ranks had bayonets in leather scabbards on a bandolier (except the sharpshooters who were equipped like the light battalion riflemen).

Line infantry officers carried their swords on white shoulder-belts called Baldrics. Pioneers, senior NCOs, musicians, and buglers carried carbines with a pouch for ten cartridges on their waistbelts.

Pioneers had short, wide, straight-bladed swords with saw-teeth along the back.

Cavalry Horse Furniture
Horse Artillery: An English saddle with blue, red-edged shabrack. Harness was brown. Drivers wore a padded wooden splint on the outside of their right legs to protect them against being crushed by the trail-pole of the limber, and carried leather whips.

Heavy Dragoons: English saddles, blue shabrack with, for the 1st Regiment black trim and the 2nd Regiment red trim. (Officers wore gold-trimmed shabracks on parade.) Harness was brown with face cross-straps, crupper and breast-straps. On conversion to light dragoons, they adopted hussar harness.

All mounted men had blue portmanteaux (the artillery drivers carried theirs on the backs of the led horses).

Hussars: Bock saddles (light, wooden Hungarian or Turkish saddles) with, at first, a shabrack, later a sheepskin. Other details as for heavy dragoons.

Cleaning materials were carried (by those with English saddles) in a leather pouch opposite to the pistol-holster, i.e. on the left. Hussars had two smaller pouches behind their holsters.

Rolled greatcoats were carried on the pommel.

A white linen haversack, blue wooden canteen forward on the saddle and a canvas feed-bag and

cooking-pot behind completed the attachments, and a picket rope was hung to the left rear of the saddle.

Infantry: Their packs were of canvas, painted in the colour of their collars, and contained underwear, washing and cleaning kit, a second pair of shoes, cloth cap and other spare clothing.

Greatcoats or blankets were rolled or folded and strapped on top of the pack. A metal cooking-cum-eating-pot was also strapped on and a canvas haversack and blue wooden canteen completed their equipment.

Pioneers carried a shovel over one shoulder with its blade in a leather case and a saw or axe over the other. They wore a white or brown leather apron.

Hair and Beards
Pigtails remained until the Peninsular campaign (1809) but the heavy dragoons retained theirs until 1812. The men of the 3rd Hussars also wore black side plaits up to and including the rank of corporal. Hussars of all ranks wore moustaches (as did light dragoons from 1813 onwards). Other troops were allowed only side whiskers. The exception to this rule was the 2nd Light Battalion (of Lieutenant-Colonel Colin Halkett) who wore moustaches throughout the battalion's existence.

Flags and Standards
Artillery, hussars and light battalions carried no colours. Each heavy dragoon regiment had one King's Standard and each of their squadrons had a guidon. Each King's Standard was crimson and square, and in the centre was a crown over the rose, thistle, and shamrock surrounded by the Garter motto. In the two corners nearest the staff were the regimental initials and the white Hanoverian horse. Both sides were identical and they were edged in gold fringes.

The squadron guidons were fork-tailed, gold-fringed; dark blue for the 1st Regiment, black for the 2nd with similar embroidery to the King's Standard. The number of the squadron appeared below the central motif. All colours were carried by the youngest cornets and stood in the centre of the regiment or squadron.

Each line battalion had a King's colour and a battalion colour. The first was a Union Jack with 'King's German Legion' within a wreath all in gold in

Colour-bearer, 5th line battalion in parade dress. He is holding the battalion flag, which is now stored in the Historisches Museum in Hanover, with other relics of the Legion. (Roffe/Osprey)

This sergeant of a Light Battalion is in 'undress' walking-out dress. Although informal it is quite smart. He carries a cane, which shows he is an NCO. NCOs no longer carry canes but officers do and they vary between different regiments. (Roffe/Osprey)

the centre, and the latter were dark blue, having the Union Jack in the top staff corner and the battalion designation, in gold, in the centre of the flag.

Battle Honours

These were worn on the shako-plates and colours. All units but the 3rd and 8th Line battalions had 'Peninsular'. All units but the 6th and 7th Line battalions and the 2nd Hussars had 'Waterloo' (16–18 June 1815).

The 3rd Hussars and the two Horse Artillery batteries had 'Gohrde' (16 September 1813).

Both heavy dragoon regiments had 'Garcia Hernandez' (23 July 1812).

Both light battalions had 'Venta del Pozo' (23 October 1812).

The 1st Hussars had 'El Bodon' (25 September 1811).

The 2nd Hussars had 'Barrossa' (5 May 1811).

These battle honours were carried by the Prussian Army descendants of these units up until 1914.

Flagstaffs were brown, flagstaff-tips brass and spearshaped and pierced to form a drooping, upright cross. Gold cords and tassels were fastened beneath the tip of the flagstaff and extended two-thirds of the way down the colour.

The Black Brunswickers

Formation

When the Duchy of Brunswick was dissolved in 1807 the son of the dead duke, the dispossessed Friedrich Wilhelm, fled to Austrian territory to nurture in exile his hatred of the French dictator.

Peace again reigned on the European mainland until 1808, but then the war in the Spanish peninsula broke out with the rejection by proud Spaniards of their new king, Joseph Bonaparte – Napoleon's brother – whom the Corsican had attempted to force on them.

Since the bitter defeats and loss of territory of 1805, Austria had been hard at work overhauling and expanding her military machine. Although much had been accomplished in this field, Archduke Charles, brother of Emperor Franz I and the man in overall charge of these army reforms, was not convinced that the Austrian forces were yet in a state to be matched against the French Army. His protests were overridden, however, as the Austrian Govern-

This gunner from a Horse Artillery battery is wearing a short black kollet *coat with six rows of black lace on the chest and three rows of black glass buttons. His leather is black but collar, shoulder-strap, coat turnbacks, and trouser stripes are light blue.*

ment felt that with the eruption of the Spanish war, Napoleon would be too occupied to be able to devote large forces to deal with them. Apart from the regular Austrian forces, extensive *Landwehr* (militia) formations had been raised, equipped, armed and semi-trained; a number of volunteer corps were also raised.

On 25 February 1809 Friedrich Wilhelm of Brunswick entered into an agreement with the Austrians to raise a corps of infantry and cavalry to fight alongside them as they invaded his old domains, raising the population against their French rulers. Initially, this corps was to consist of an infantry regiment and a hussar regiment each of 1,000 men. The infantry regiment was organized in two battalions each of four companies and the hussar

This private in a Line Battalion is in field service marching order. His black uniform has a white collar and shoulder-straps and white piping on the trouser seams.

regiment had eight squadrons. The hussar regiment had a horse artillery battery attached to it consisting of two light 7-pounder howitzers and two light 6-pounder cannon.

To set the new corps on its feet the Austrian Government provided the following items:

1,000 infantry shakos
1,000 hussar shakos
1,000 pairs of shoes
1,000 pairs of hussar boots (*Czismen*)
1,000 pairs of spurs
1,000 hussar-pattern waistbelts
1,000 cavalry cartridge pouches
1,000 infantry cartridge pouches
1,000 infantry overcoats

1,000 sets of hussar-pattern harness
1,000 carbines
1,000 infantry muskets with slings
1,000 brace of pistols
The cloth (pepper-and-salt mixture) for 1,000 cavalry greatcoats
2 light 7-pounder howitzers with all accessories
2 light 6-pounder cannon with all accessories
8 ammunition wagons and 240 rounds for each gun, together with the necessary case-shot cartridges
240 rounds of ammunition per head for each infantryman and cavalryman
12,000 musket flints
12,000 pistol flints
25 *Windbüchsen*   (This was a repeating air rifle capable of firing 12 rounds at an effective range of about 200 paces, almost noiselessly, before requiring a recharged air cylinder. For its era it was a very advanced weapon, invented by Girardoni but it required skilful maintenance and after Girardoni's death it fell into disuse.)

The town of Nachod in Bohemia was selected as the forming-up place for the Brunswick Corps and on 1 April 1809 both the infantry and cavalry regiments assembled for the first time.

The dispossessed Friedrich Wilhelm of Brunswick was totally concerned with the idea of revenge against Napoleon for the damage which had been done to his family and lands. As a physical expression of this vengeance he decided to clothe his new troops all in black and adopted as his badge the skull and crossbones. As a result he became known as *Der Schwarzer Herzog* (the Black Duke) and his corps was christened *Die Schwarze Schar* (the Black Horde).

Numbers in Different Campaigns
On attempting the overthrow of Westphalia, the Black Duke had the following force:

Infantry (Commander: Oberst von Bernewitz)

1st Battalion	500 men under Major von Fragstein
2nd Battalion	500 men under Major von Reichmeister
3rd Battalion	150 men under Major von Herzberg
Scharfschützen	150 men under Major von Scriever

Cavalry

Hussars	550 men; the regiment was commanded by Major Schrader as the *Oberstleutnant*. Von Steinmann was recovering from a wound
Uhlanen	80 men under *Rittmeister* Graf von Wedell

Artillery (Premier-Leutnant Genderer)

4 guns	80 men

Total: 100 officers and 2,010 men

The general uprising that the Duke had counted on as he pushed towards Brunswick did not occur, so he made a getaway to England, from whence the Black Horde went next to fight in the Peninsula.

The Infantry

On 8 October 1810 the Brunswick-Oels Jägers, as the infantry regiment was then known, landed at Lisbon. They were apparently twelve companies and a regimental headquarters strong, and initially went to Pakenham's Brigade in Cole's 4th Division. Shortly after this they were transferred to General Craufurd's Light Division and, as part of this formation, they took part in the pursuit of Marshal Masséna from the Lines of Torres Vedras on 17 November 1810, and in the skirmish at Santarém (19 November). Other actions in which they participated in the Light Division were Redinka (12 March 1811), Casal Novo (14 March), and Foz d'Arouce (16 March).

After this they were transferred from the Light Division to the newly-formed 7th Division which they joined before April 1811. They were in von Alten's Brigade with a strength of the regimental HQ and nine companies, the other companies being detached as follows: 4th Division (General Lowry Cole), one company in Ellis's Brigade; 5th Division (General Leith), one company in Greville's Brigade, and one company in Pringle's Brigade. The officers commanding these formations changed too frequently during the war to set them out here.

The main body of the Jägers (still in the 7th Division) was engaged in the battles of the Nivelle (10 November) and the Nive (9 December). The company in the 5th Division also had losses in this latter battle and on the next day. Their last battle in the Peninsular campaign was that of Orthez on 27 February 1814 where the Brunswickers in the 7th Division were quite heavily involved. The strength of the main body of the Brunswick-Oels Jägers in the 7th Division at the battle of the Nivelle was forty-two officers and 457 men.

An example of the stylish and shaped short coat worn by the lancers of the Brunswick Corps.

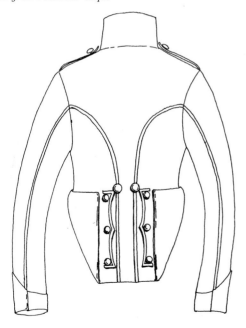

Officer, Horse Artillery in parade dress, which included the British 'light dragoon' helmet and hussar-pattern dolman and pelisse. (Roffe/Osprey)

LOSSES OF THE BRUNSWICK-OELS JÄGERS IN THE PENINSULA

Battle and Date	Parent formation	KILLED		WOUNDED		MISSING		Total
		Officers	Men	Officers	Men	Officers	Men	
Fuentes d'Onoro 5 May 1811	7th Division	–	1	1	6	–	10	18
Siege of Badajoz 9 June 1811	7th Division	–	1	1	5	–	–	7
Siege of Badajoz 6 April 1812	4th Division / 5th Division	–	7	2	26	–	–	35
Battle of Vitoria 21 June 1813	4th Division / 5th Division / 7th Division	1	–	–	5	–	–	6
Battle of Maya 25 July 1813	7th Division	–	8	3	15	–	15	41
Roncesvalles 25 July 1813	4th Division	–	2	–	2	–	–	4
1st Sorauren 28 July 1813	4th Division	–	1	–	3	–	1	5
2nd Sorauren 30 July 1813	7th Division	–	2	–	1	–	14	17
Skirmish at Echalar 2 Aug. 1813	7th Division	–	1	4	7	–	2	14
Siege of San Sebastian 31 Aug. 1813	5th Division	–	2	1	6	1	5	15
Crossing of the Bidassoa 7 Oct. 1813	1st Division / 4th Division	–	7	7	18	–	–	32
Battle of the Nive 9 Dec. 1813	5th Division	–	2	–	1	–	1	4
10 Dec. 1813	5th Division	–	–	1	2	–	–	3
11 Dec. 1813	5th Division	–	1	1	1	–	–	3
Battle of Orthez 27 Feb, 1814	7th Division	2	5	5	32	–	4	48
Totals		3	40	26	130	1	52	252

The Hussars

The cavalry of the Black Horde were reorganized into a regiment of hussars which was also sent to Spain, but to the eastern side of the Peninsula where they operated in a force made up largely of foreign levies which was used in amphibious operations along the Spanish coast. This force was commanded by Sir John Murray and included English, Portuguese, Spanish, and Italian troops.

The Brunswick Hussars, two squadrons strong, landed at Alicante, direct from England, in July 1813. First they took part in the badly managed raid on Tarragona. Then on 25 August 1813 the Brunswick Hussars, with eighteen officers and 258 troopers,

The officer on the left is talking to one of his lancers. The officer's trousers have twin light blue stripes whereas lancers had only one.

became part of Lord Bentinck's Brigade in this British force on the east coast of Spain. At the combat of Villa Franca on 13 September 1813, they were engaged and lost one officer and eight men, with two officers and twenty-four men wounded and eighteen men missing. In 1814 they took part in the invasion of Sicily.

The sergeant on the right is giving orders to Jägers *of the Leib-Bataillon. Note the rolled overcoat of the sharpshooters who may have to lie up for a lengthy period.*

The Brunswick-Oels *Jägers* returned home and left English service on 25 December 1814, but their hussar colleagues remained in English service until mid-1815.

When the Russian and Prussian armies had flooded across north Germany in 1813, the Duke of Brunswick-Oels had been confirmed in his family possessions and at once set about raising new forces which could be used to speed Napoleon's downfall. The first unit raised was a company of *Gelernte Jäger* which was completed on 1 January 1814. By 16 March 1814 a second company had been formed. Before the year was out Brunswick's forces were:

LEICHTE-INFANTERIE-BRIGADE

1.   The Avantgarde: The original infantry of the Black Horde now returned from English service, and the two new Gelernte Jäger companies. There was a total of four companies in the Avantgarde

2.   The Leib-Bataillon: A new Leib-Bataillon

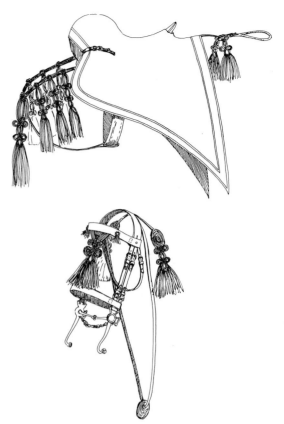

Three privates, discussing Higher Strategy, perhaps. On the right a hussar, in the centre a light infantryman, and on the left a member of a rifle company.

Two officers and a mounted trooper in a Uhlan squadron. Note the elaborate headgear.

The ornamental shabrack and harness shown in these illustrations was used by Hussar and Uhlan officers, and was partly designed to discourage flies.

raised from a cadre of the Black Horde and initially known as the 'Leichte-Bataillon von Pröstler' (the name of its commander); on 14 April 1815 this unit became known as the 'Leib-Bataillon'

3. *1st, 2nd and 3rd Leichte-Bataillone:* Newly-raised troops

LINIEN-INFANTERIE-BRIGADE
4. *1st, 2nd, and 3rd, Linien-Infanterie-Bataillone:* Newly-raised troops

RESERVE-INFANTERIE-BRIGADE
5. *1st, 2nd, 3rd, 4th and 5th Reserve-Infanterie-Bataillone,* and a type of *Lanwehr*

HUSAREN-REGIMENT
6. This included a squadron of *Uhlanen* and all men were newly-raised troops

This trooper in a hussar regiment has brass chin scales on his helmet, a black dolman with light blue collar and cuffs, and a yellow cord waist-sash with light blue barrels. (Roffe/Osprey)

ARTILLERIE

7.   One foot battery – 8 guns
      One horse artillery battery
      8 guns   } Newly-raised troops
      The military train

   Apart from the hussars quoted above, the old

This uniform is a mixture of styles and is worn by a sharpshooter. He has no badge but a very practical stalker's hat, a black satchel, a sling to his rifle, and trousers which were usually greyer with dirt than appears here. (Roffe/Osprey)

hussars of the original Black Horde were still in English service. The foot artillery battery had 188 men and the horse artillery battery 227. With the exception of the Reserve-Infanterie-Brigade, these forces were present at Quatre Bras and at Waterloo.

   The Brunswicker contingent at Quatre Bras consisted of the following:

The Avantgarde

Two companies of Gelernte Jäger
                                       }   690 men
Two companies of light infantry

This trooper in English service is dressed in practical style with breeches tucked into his boots and minimum decoration lest his movements should be impeded. (Roffe/Osprey)

This sergeant in the Lieb-Bataillon is wearing the infantry shako with the drooping horsehair plume, silver rank chevrons, and a sabre with a light blue knot. Sergeants and above wore white gloves. (Roffe/Osprey)

The Line Infantry Brigade
1st Line Infantry Battalion
2nd Line Infantry Battalion } 2,075 men
3rd Line Infantry Battalion

The Cavalry
The Hussar Regiment } 727 men
Uhlan Squadron } 246 men

The Light Infantry Brigade
The Leib-Bataillon
1st Light Infantry Battalion
2nd Light Infantry Battalion } 2,965 men
3rd Light Infantry Battalion

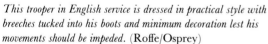

This dolman and waistcoat of a subaltern of the Lieb-Bataillon shows the embroidery, which is black on the blue collar of the dolman and silver on the blue collar of the waistcoat.

The Artillery

One horse artillery battery of 8 guns	188 men
One foot artillery battery of 8 guns	227 men

The Feldgendarmerie

One commando of Polizei-Husaren	17 men

The official Brunswick dispatch concerning the battle, gives the casualty figures for Quatre Bras as follows:

	Killed	Wounded	Total
Officers	3	23	26
Men	185	373	558
	188	396	584

No mention is made of missing personnel.

The Black Duke was killed trying to re-form his men at Quatre Bras and was succeeded by Oberst Olfermann.

The whole of the Brunswick Corps was present at Waterloo, beginning the battle in the Allied reserve, but soon being committed to action. The strength of the corps, according to Siborne, was:

Infantry	4,586
Cavalry	866
Artillery	510 with 16 guns
	5,962

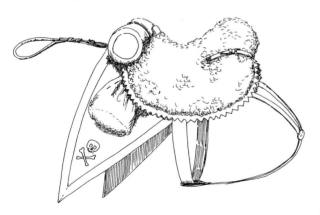

This hussar's saddle has a sheepskin cover with a light blue, wolf's-tooth edge. Note the white death's-head badge. The harness is black with brass fittings.

The Duke of Brunswick – the Black Duke – who clothed his troops in black as a symbol of the vengeance he would wreak on Napoleon for the damage he had caused.

*A hussar trooper of the Black Horde (*Die Schwarze Schar*). His long off-white greatcoat is in sharp contrast to the rest of his attire.*

This sergeant-major of the 1st Line Infantry Battalion has four silver chevrons to denote his rank and also carries his stick of office.

This trooper in the Uhlan squadron has a smaller version of the skull-and-crossbones badge and wears dark green in Polish style. Note that his chapka is yellow at the top. (Roffe/Osprey)

The soldier here is serving in an infantry regiment in English service. His shako is distinctive but most of his kit, including the BLJ canteen and Brown Bess, is British. (Roffe/Osprey)

The sharpshooter comes from an infantry regiment in the English service. His shako is standard Brunswicker infantry pattern and his clothing is practical. He has a Baker rifle and a short sword-bayonet. (Roffe/Osprey)

The officer of the Lieb-Bataillon carries no equipment but is also distinguished by yellow and silver waist-sash. He carries a cavalry sabre. (Roffe/Osprey)

The driver of foot artillery has an artillery shako, an infantry tunic, and a brass-hilted sabre. He wears a black bandolier and pouch. (Roffe/Osprey)

The Brunswickers were split into three parts for the duration of Waterloo. The cavalry operated with other Allied cavalry units. The Avantgarde, the Lieb-Bataillon, and the 1st Light Battalion were posted at the north-west corner of Hougoumont, in support of the garrison there, and the 2nd and 3rd Light Battalions and the three line battalions, together with the artillery, were initially in reserve in the second line of the Allied position. The garrison of Hougoumont consisted of Byng's Guards Brigade. Their

The sergeant-major hardly needs the authority conferred by his four chevrons, crown, and white gloves. His personality is almost as compelling as his rank badges. (Roffe/Osprey)

immediate opponents on the western half of the battlefield were once again to be the forces under Ney, with whom they had fought so desperately at Quatre Bras only two days before.

Siborne gives the losses of the Brunswickers at Waterloo as:

	Killed	Wounded	Missing
Officers	7	26	–
NCOs and men	147	430	50
Horses	77	–	–

The Germans in general received high praise for their conduct at Waterloo, particularly the King's German Legion and some of the Hanoverians. The Brunswickers had their fair share of this glory, justly won and paid for in the blood they shed in those few momentous days in 1815.

The Brunswick troops later formed the 92nd Infantry Regiment and the 17th Hussar Regiment of the Prussian Army from 1866 to 1918.

The death's-head badge was retained as the cap-badge of the Brunswick Hussars as were the battle honours won during the period 1809–15 namely: 'Peninsula' and 'Waterloo'.

There were thus three hussar regiments in the German Army of 1914–18 who wore a skull-and-crossbones badge; these were the 1st and 2nd Regiments of Leibhusaren and the Brunswickers.

A captain in a Line battalion wearing service dress. The waist-sash and sabre-strap are silver and gold. The plume is blue and yellow feathers and the trouser stripes provide yet another contrast.

The private in the Line battalion has a badge composed of a silver hunting-horn and the regimental number. His shako pompom is yellow over light blue. His facings are orange. (Roffe/Osprey)

The senior musician of a Line battalion has the gold facing colour which denotes his rank but wears the standard infantry shako. He carries a sabre but no other arms. (Roffe/Osprey)

INDEX